DARE TO BE A

DIFFERENCE
Maker

Volume 4

DARE TO BE A DIFFERENCE Maker

Volume 4

DIFFERENCE MAKERS WHO DARE TO LIVE
WITH PASSION, FOLLOW THEIR PURPOSE
AND COMMIT TO HELPING OTHERS!

MICHELLE PRINCE

Dedication

To all the "Difference Makers" in the world
who are making a difference by following your heart.
Thanks for letting your "light" shine!

Introduction

For many years as I worked in "Corporate America", I would say to myself "I just want to make a difference!" I was selling software and I'm sure I was making some difference for my clients but not in the way I wanted to. I wanted to help, serve, encourage and motivate people. I wanted to make a positive impact on their lives but I didn't know how...how could just one person really make a significant difference? So I didn't...for a long time. I continued to work in an area that wasn't my passion or calling. I didn't follow my heart and God's promptings to go in the direction of my purpose and dreams. Instead, I just let year after year go by feeling unfulfilled unhappy and spiritually broken.

That is, until one day in 2008 when I had my "aha" moment. It hit me like a ton of bricks that it's my responsibility to follow my passions and purpose. No one can do that for me. I took action to write my first book, *Winning In Life Now*, began to speak, motivate and mentor others to live their best life and, as they say, "the rest is history."

What I found over this journey is that we all have a desire to make a difference. We all want to live with passion and follow our God-given callings; our purpose. It's through this understanding that I decided to write this series of books.

Dare To Be A Difference Maker 4, is my vision to have a unique collection of narratives, not only from inspired leaders, but also from those I see making a difference and impacting others in their everyday personal and professional life. These stories are about *real* people who are making a *real* difference even on a small scale.

My mission in creating the "Difference Maker Movement" and in writing the series of *Dare To Be A Difference Maker* books is that you will gain inspiration, wisdom and the courage you need in order to get through life's tough challenges and make a difference for others in the process.

So many people I speak with these days discuss their issues as though they are losing hope. It is my vision for this book to reach the masses and have a powerful effect on people in their everyday lives. It is my prayer that this book, and all the volumes, will breathe new life into your mind and spirit and that it will inspire you to take action in order to help others.

I've selected an exclusive group of difference-makers who I know can motivate, inspire and be a part of a movement to change people's lives. Everyone can do this; it just takes commitment and honoring of our unique and sacred gifts. It is to those people, I dedicate this book.

From one "Difference Maker" to another,

Michelle

P.S. Do you or anyone you know have a story about making a difference? We are currently interviewing authors for our next book and would love to have you join us in this amazing journey. To submit an entry, please contact Info@Prince Performance.com for more details. While one powerful story can be fascinating many can move mountains!

Table of Contents

Fairytales, Fate, and Fortitude
Kimberly Alexander

He kept complaining about his feet hurting. His legs ached. But he kept going. He went to doctors; he visited specialists; no one could find anything wrong with him. "You've played football for years," they would say. "This is normal." My husband was 35 years old. After years of little league, high school, college, and professional football, yes, it was plausible that his feet hurt—just because. So he carried on. Then things spiraled, quickly, unexpectedly, like a tornado.

It was an emergency room doctor who diagnosed him. After all the physicians he'd visited in prior months, after all the years of being given physicals by the professional teams he played for, it was a young doctor with whom we just happened to cross paths who would enlighten us and devastate us at the same time. When he first entered the tiny emergency room bay the doctor let us know he was supposed to be getting off from work soon. It was after midnight at this point, and I had our two sons at home being watched by a friend. My husband sent me home; he was stable; he wanted me to get some rest and come back in the morning. After all, the doctor said he'd have some tests run and it'd be a while before the results would be known. So I left him, with a kiss on his forehead and a kiss on his lips.

Like any typical mom, I woke up the next morning to get breakfast for our sons and get them off to school, all while trying to dodge the

"Where's dad?" question. They were nine and seven years old at that time; I needed to keep them happy and carefree. Drop them off, get gas, get back to the hospital—that was my "to do"list for the day. He called me just as the nozzle on the gas pump clicked letting me know the tank was full. I don't even think I said hello. I answered the phone with a question, "What'd they say?" That's all I wanted to know. What did they say? "They" being the test results, "they" being the doctors, "they" being the nurses, "they" being anyone who could explain to me what made my husband utter the words, "I think I'm dying" not even 12 hours earlier.

He wouldn't answer my question though. I stood in the drive of that gas station waiting for him to say something satisfying, but all I kept getting was avoidance. I noticed it. I interpreted it. It didn't make me not repeat my question though. And again, he ignored me. In return, he asked me, "When will you be coming back to the hospital? I need you to sign some paperwork." I tried to pick up on something in his tone, longing to hear him say, "Oh, it's nothing; they gave me a prescription and are ready to check me out!" But that never came. After telling him I was on my way, I called my dad and had a complete meltdown. He was living in Florida. We'd seen him just six months earlier when we renewed our wedding vows for our ten-year anniversary. My dad tried to say all the right things, but I knew it didn't matter because the one I needed to hear those things from gave me everything but.

I don't remember parking; I don't remember walking through the emergency room entrance; I just remember how brightly the sun illuminated his room, which just the night before was dark with glowing red and green lights from all the machinery hooked up to him monitoring his stats. I looked him in the face still longing for a clue as to what happened during those hours I was at home tending to our boys. He wouldn't look at me. Instead he handed me a clipboard filled with papers and a pen. *This is just like old times, right?* That's what I thought. He never liked filling out papers or signing anything, so I always did. He knew I drew the line at signing football cards, though—he'd autograph those. We all have limits. It was just a given that everything else was my duty. I'm convinced he had that implanted in our vows somewhere the first go round, "To have and to hold, to fill out papers you don't want to bother with…."

So I get started on the paperwork. I'm not noticing anything alarming from what I'm reading, but I'm wondering, "Why do we need more paperwork done?" I ask again, "What did the doctor say?" The two words that followed were the two words I never expected to hear. It seemed like the earth stopped spinning on its axis just for me to process them. "It's cancer." I was leaning up against a wall, looking at him, blinking, thinking, breathing, repeating his words in my head. And then I snapped out of it—"it" being a momentary trance that seemed like eternity. In that moment, I took his words, assumed his condition, determined his treatment, and knew his prognosis. I had it all figured out and immediately switched into fight mode, because flight was not an option—not for us, not for me. It's cancer so that means the doctor will cut it out; he'll get some chemotherapy and be just fine. People get diagnosed with cancer all the time; people beat cancer all the time; let's roll.

My mind stopped racing just long enough for me to ask the next logical question. I looked over at him lying in the bed, the man I'd been with since I was 19 years old, the man I'd been married to for 10 years, the man who fathered my children, the man whose 6'3", 235-lb. frame allowed him to live his childhood dream of being a linebacker in the NFL, and he looked shattered. "What kind of cancer?" I asked. He responded, "myeloma." Skin cancer? Wait, no, that's not it. I made a mad dash for the computer in the room so I could go to Google and try to understand what he was saying to me. I don't remember him talking much after that. It was probably a good thing because what I read about the disease put me right back into a state of shock. The words "terminal," "incurable," "blood cancer," "affects most people in their 60s and 70s," "patients usually die within four to five years" hit me all at once. How could this be?

Life is so funny. I distinctly remember sitting at a traffic light in our perfect little town months before my husband's cancer diagnosis thinking, "Wow, our lives have been so smooth." We did everything by the book. I was the planner. Everything we did revolved around his foot-ball career from the very beginning. I met him after his rookie season when I was a sophomore in college. When the business side of the game abruptly moved him across the country to a new team, I broke my dad's heart and moved too.

We became engaged, I enrolled in school in our new city and got a job. Then came wedding planning and family planning—all around the NFL schedule. July through January was owned by whichever team he played for that season. February through June was our downtime. That's how it was throughout his ten-year career. Throw in an injury, a few surgeries, lots of rehab, two baby boys, and bouncing from team to team, and I became proficient at juggling. Any thoughts of using my journal-ism degree faded fast. No one wanted to hire someone who moves every six months. So I embraced being his wife and their mom. My men need-ed me to hold down the fort, regardless of which state it was in.

When my husband decided to hang up his cleats, he had my full support. His plans for life after football were already in motion. During his last football season I started a T-shirt business that I kept and ex-panded, even after we settled into our permanent home. He became a little league football coach. I became more involved with charity work and hosted luncheons for local active and retired NFL wives. Everything was smooth sailing. The transition out of football was effortless, unlike what the statistics typically report. And within three years of him retiring from football we had the rug snatched out from under us.

He'd tell me all the time not to ask, "Why us?" The question really should have been, "Why not us?" So I adopted that attitude and dove into discovering all things myeloma—I wanted to know. I was 32 years old and having to come to terms with the fact that those dreams of grow-ing old with my husband, sitting in a swing on a porch while watching our grandchildren play in the yard, may not happen. He always said he wanted to live long enough to see our sons graduate from high school. I knew there was a chance I might be raising them alone. However, I wanted to keep things normal—as normal as you can when the head of your household needs care because of a cancer diagnosis.

Remarkably, he flourished as a cancer patient. I shouldn't even refer to him as one. He was more like a warrior. While recovering from a stem cell transplant he declared he wanted to start a charity for young cancer patients, and that's what he did. He took on speaking engagements and became very involved with the cancer community. I sat back and marveled. The way his cancer worked was that it would go into remission and then come back. It was something that he could live with for years because so many advancements were made around the time he was diagnosed. He had his ups and downs. The public saw him when he was up—I saw him both ways. Being a caregiver meant that most times I was on autopilot. I felt as if I had to be Wonder Woman and use magical wrist cuffs to make sure he was as healthy as possible and our sons were as happy as possible. That meant playing preventive defense, keeping my head on a swivel to make sure he wasn't overdoing it, making sure the boys weren't coming home from school with simple germs that could bring him to his knees, all the while trying to maintain a hint of sanity at the same time.

One morning it became painfully clear that all the planning in the world cannot ever prepare you for fate. There are things that are simply beyond our control. While we both knew what having myeloma meant and assumed that would be what would take him, we found ourselves sucker punched. Just shy of his five-year anniversary of life with myeloma, I lost my husband to a brain aneurysm. I was literally talking to him one minute and 20 minutes later he was gone. Gone! The plans we had for watching his alma mater in the Sweet 16 didn't matter. His wanting to see our sons march across a stage in their caps and gowns didn't matter. Our wanting to play with grandchildren would simply never happen. At 37 years of age I was a widow, a single mom with two middle-school-aged sons. Our boys had been robbed. We were so preoccupied with myeloma that the complications of life with it, such as the blood clots we just saw as nuisances, never seemed life-threatening. But they were! They were life-threatening, life-altering, life-shattering, life-ending. And here I was with those same options again, fight versus flight.

My husband was gone, but I knew his two gifts to me needed me in the worst way. If I collapsed, who would our sons turn to? So collapsing was not an option. Holding everything together regardless of how much I wanted to fall apart was the only way I could go. I had to set an example. I had to think, "What would he want me to do?" So I kept my head held high, wept privately, and encouraged our sons to move forward. I never wanted them to use the loss of their father as an excuse to backslide. But I knew they would be watching me so I had to practice what I preached.

Losing my husband made me realize that I'd lived life in a little cocoon. Being forced to change and establish life with a set of new normals meant experiencing lots of uncomfortable moments. I now equate those moments with growth and manage to find a bright side in every situation. It also made me realize how precious time is and how much people take life and relationships for granted. I used to tell people that becoming a widow didn't change me. But it did, greatly. My perspective has been altered. While I once believed, "There's always a next time," "I can do it later," that is, quite simply, no longer the case. I keep a bucket list a mile long, and once I scratch something off it I add something new to it. The one thing I never added, but knew I needed to make sure I did, was that from that point forward whatever I decided to do needed to be something that made me happy, because life is too short.

Life never stopped moving when my world crumbled. The juggling act didn't end; in fact, the pins just changed, and then increased in number. But I was equipped with a new outlook and a set of challenges that forced me to rediscover things I'd forgotten about myself over the years. Progressing from student to wife, from wife to mom, from wife, mom, and caregiver to widowed mom, allowed for many "ah ha" moments. I'd lost *me* in the shuffle and had never even realized it. It became time to remember, regroup, and reinvent. Moving forward would require this.

Now, experiences mean more to me than moments. Deep connections and relationships mean more than just being able to say I know someone. I look at everyone; I look at everything; and I wonder what's beyond the surface. We've all had our challenges. Many of us are con-nected by them, and sometimes we don't even realize it. But I do. I tell people all the time that I will never fix my lips to complain about what I've experienced. Instead, I take my experiences and share them with the hope that it makes people realize the importance of being happy and joyful, when it matters, while we are still here. ■

KIMBERLY ALEXANDER *owns Kim-CONNECTS, a boutique consulting firm that specializes in small-business development, social media, project management, and private events. Known for her "little purple book," she utilizes her connections to create opportunities for clients. Alexander also co-hosts "The GAME" with Timm Matthews, a Dallas-based sports radio talk show on 105.3 FM. In 2010, Kimberly lost her husband, former NFL linebacker Elijah Alexander, to complications due to multiple myeloma, an incurable blood cancer. As a result of that experience she is now involved with several nonprofit organizations; these include the International Myeloma Foundation, the Leukemia and Lymphoma Society (North Texas chapter) and St. Jude Children's Research Hospital. She was also a founding board member of the Off the Field Players' Wives Association. As an advocate for cancer-related initiatives, she narrated an educational video entitled, "Multiple Myeloma in the African American Community", has co-hosted oncology-related events and been a guest speaker on the topic.*

Kimberly Alexander
KimConnects
5729 Lebanon Rd.
Ste. 144- PMB347
Frisco, TX 75034
Info@KimConnects.com

Who Am I?

Cody Barton

When I first thought about possibly writing a book, it was always something that got me excited, but I thought you had to be a certain kind of person to do it. So from the beginning, when I was first thinking about writing this chapter and putting it together, I always shut myself down on the idea. Even as I've been working on it, going through the process, it was always something that I was timid about doing. I didn't really believe that I had it in me to do it and I was scared what other people were going to think or what other people would say behind my back, and things like that. I knew my grammar wasn't the best when I was going through school and my flow with words wasn't the best. I remember my teachers always telling me that, and it drew my confidence away from even starting.

The real reason I just had to get this story out, and that you have to read this, and the reason I feel this is so important is this: I realize that I've gleaned information from multiple sources, from other authors to motivational speakers to different mentors I've had. I have a big collection of stuff just rambling around in my head, and I truly feel it will benefit so many people. So my purpose for this entire chapter is not to impress but, instead, to give people something of value for their life. I plan to pass on to you some information that I've been given and that's benefited my life in a positive way.

I want to start off by saying that I am writing this to educate you on taking steps toward your goals, toward starting up your own organization or your own business. If you don't already know my story, let me begin by describing exactly who I am. Growing up, I always viewed myself as very different from everybody else, almost like a black sheep when it came to my mindset. I made friends pretty easily, but I was the kid in class always making the teachers upset. Was I a bad student? I don't believe so. I just thought differently. I just had questions, and people don't like it when you ask too many questions. They like you to take the information and just deal with the way things are. I didn't like that and often voiced my opinion.

I was the kid who would question every topic or lesson we would learn. Why are we learning this? How is the Pythagorean theorem relevant—whatever it is—and why do I care if Jimmy has 20 apples and five friends and how many ways he could split them between the friends? I honestly don't care. I didn't understand that. Why were we learning things that didn't apply to my life, that didn't apply to things I specifically wanted to do, and that were things I wasn't interested in? Why wasn't I learning how to make money? Why weren't we taught that? Why weren't we learning how to do taxes in school? Why weren't we learning how to balance a checkbook? Why weren't we learning how to start a business? Why were we not learning how to set goals and doing all those so very important things in life? I know all teachers and educators mean well, and I really appreciate what they do, but a lot of the things they taught just never made sense to me. Maybe you can relate to this, or maybe you know someone who was like this.

You know the teachers' responses all too well: "You need to know this because it'll be on your test." Or "You need to know this because I said so." Wait! What? I don't understand that. I started developing a different mindset early on from different mini-experiences. Both of my parents transitioned from working jobs to becoming self-employed. And that's how I've transitioned; I made the switch from the employee mindset to the entrepreneur mindset. And—lucky me!—from the ripe age of nine years old, my dad started taking me to work. By the way, my dad did manual labor. He owns a carpet, tile, and grout restoration company. I learned a lot of valuable things from watching him.

Two things I learned: Number one, manual labor sucks. Number two, I learned from watching him to always provide value to people and that it's important to treat people well. Ever since I was little he would tell me that it is quality over quantity; never sacrifice quality in what you do. When you do this you are able to gain a great reputation.

This mindset led me into my first entrepreneurial pursuit, which happened when I was 15 years old. I found a wholesale Chinese distributor online—basically, they sold a rubber bracelet. I'm not going to mention the name, but it promised people that it would help them balance better, be stronger, faster, and perform better. Being an athlete, the light bulb went on in my head because that interested me. I found that the bracelets normally sold for about $30 a band, but the site I found was selling these bands for about 97 cents apiece. So, being a 15-year-old ready to make some money, I saw dollar signs immediately. I got stoked and bought 100 bands; I spent about $97. So I made my first order and started selling them for about $20 a band to my friends, to various athletes. I would even set up booths at school programs. I hustled these bands all over the place, and they started selling like wild fire.

I quickly sold the entire first batch. But for my second round, I didn't want to do all the work anymore. So this is what I did. I started by buying 100 bands for $97. At that point, I decided to find other people to work for me, other distributors. I had a few friends who wanted to make money too, so I thought, here's what I'll do. I don't want to go and sell them band by band anymore. I'm going to sell ten apiece to these other kids at a rate of, say, ten for $100. I'd sell each of them ten bands for $100, and then they'd be stoked because then they could go out and start selling them themselves. And they'd go out and sell them for whatever amount of money they wanted. I would buy 100 bands, sell ten bands each to ten different kids, and I'd be making $1,000 on the sales to these kids.

I was pretty excited. I felt like I was getting rich. The day finally came when the other kids found out where I was buying the bands and start-ed buying them through the same website instead of through me. My career selling bands was over. So I learned from that experience that it's much better to have other people working for you and doing the work. You start off with the initial money, and you get other people to do the work for you rather than you doing it all by yourself—use other people to do the work. That venture got me excited about future things I could do in the way of entrepreneurism.

The next big opportunity came to me when I was 15 years old. I remember it like it was yesterday. A direct sales company approached me, and it was such a huge deal for me because I had never seen the industry before. I had never understood entrepreneurism; I was never taught about it at home or in school. I got invited to this pool party over the summer, and I was excited about going with a couple of my really good friends. It was a well-known neighborhood called "Circle G," beau-tiful custom homes. When we pulled into the neighborhood, I remem-ber walking up to this massive front door with beautiful designs on it. It was stunning; it looked like a house out of a magazine. We went into the house, and that's when things got weird really quick.

There were lots of adults, and my reaction was, "Wait, I thought this was a pool party." There were all these old people in there and just a few younger kids. I was wondering what I had just walked into. They had a PowerPoint up in the living room, which confused me, but they had free food too so I stuck around. I ate some food, and then they had me sit down to prepare to listen to the presentation. The couple up front were so friendly, welcoming, and some of the most genuine people I had ever met. By the end of the presentation I was stoked! But then they were pushing this piece of paper in front of me to sign up. "You have to sign up with us."

It cost something like $400 to sign up, and then I had to pay a month-ly fee. It was a travel company where I had to get my friends to buy exotic trips all over the world for discounted prices. My thought process went like this: "I'm 15 years old. I don't really think my 15-year-old friends' parents are going to appreciate me trying to get their kids to buy trips to Cabo and all these places around the world. Plus, I don't really have a bunch of cash on me to actually do this." So, in the end, it didn't stick with me. I didn't get involved, but, the thing is, after checking that out, the concept was really appealing to me. I realized it was just that specific idea that wasn't for me.

As soon as I turned 16 years old, my parents got me my first car, a 2000 Jeep Cherokee—and then they hit me with this statement: "Now you need to go and get a job." They told me that while I was sitting around thinking how miserable it was going to be working for someone else. Thinking back to my experience at school, I realized even then that I just did not want to have a job. One of the biggest indicators for me was this test called an aptitude test. The test's purpose was to see what career was most likely the best fit for me when I finished school. I finished this test; I answered all the questions; and I was literally the only one in my entire class with zero results.

Every single question required that I work for somebody else and not make the money I wanted to. Every single question required that I do things I didn't want to do and sacrifice this and that, and I didn't want to do that. You can bet the teacher was not happy. She said that I didn't take the test seriously. I said, "Well, I don't want to have a job ever in my life." She just laughed and said, "Ha ha ha. How do you expect to ever make any money?"

You can already see how I felt on this subject. I knew from observing my parents that you don't need a job to make money. Still, my parents enforced this idea and said I needed a job. I was thinking, "Well, this sucks. I want to do anything but that." So the search was on. I am not sure why but I had a hard time getting a job. I applied at 29 places; I put in my application and did all the right things.

I would call the managers, follow up, go in person, and turn in application after application. I would meet the manager, shake their hand and introduce myself, and try to show them how great of a person I am. I would turn in my resume and repeatedly not get the job. Then, my last resort, the Mac Shack, better known as McDonald's, is where I got hired for the first time. I realized I wasn't making enough money there, so I got another job sign spinning in the wonderful Arizona sun. The most frustrating part of having two jobs was that most of my friends' parents paid for them to have all the things that my parents made me pay for—the car, my insurance, my gas, my fun, things like that.

Looking back now, I see working those jobs as a great lesson because it made me have to find an alternative if I wanted to achieve a different result. What is funny now is that I had to apply at so many places to get one job, whereas now I'll receive calls from different places, sales positions at different corporations that want to hire me to come work for them. Obviously, I would never do that because the whole purpose of being an entrepreneur is not working for somebody else. The way I saw everything was that my parents weren't being fair. I would be working at McDonald's or at my other job sign spinning almost every single day while my friends went out, had fun, got to drive their cars that their parents paid for, along with the gas, and go out on their parents' money.

The freedom that I saw they had become one of my biggest motivations. I didn't quite have a vehicle yet to escape my situation. Looking at it all, I knew there was one other option, which was, "OK, get another job somewhere else." And, I mean, that wasn't a very good option because that still wouldn't give me the time and freedom I wanted. One day—this is like the magical day that everything in my life changed—one tiny thing changed my entire life. My sister approached me with this health and wellness company that had a similar concept to the direct sales company that I was introduced to a couple of years before when I was 15. I was immediately interested. I actually tried one of the products, a healthy energy drink, and I loved it. But I didn't see the big picture; I wasn't ready to get started right away.

I sat on it for a little while. A couple of weeks went by as I was researching the company. I found so many people who were becoming so absolutely disgustingly wealthy and creating this freedom through direct sales and network marketing. For me it was just like, "What the heck?

How are all these normal people doing this?" The light bulb flashed on in my head: "This is the way out." This is how I'm supposed to get out of my job right now.

So I got started, and I expected instant success. Boy, I was wrong. I signed up and got started, but I didn't really get trained correctly; I didn't really understand it; I didn't have a mentor. Neither did my sister. We were just doing it. I would sign up friend after friend after friend because my friends listened to me when it came to making money. I would just say, "Yo, we're going to make a lot of money with this. We're going to take this thing to the top. We're going to be so successful." And they would all sign up, and they were all expecting instant gratification.

I realized it wasn't going to happen that way. I stayed and realized this was for the long term because I'd seen other people do it. But over and over my friends just quit. They'd be quitting over and over—quitting, quitting, quitting. But all I had to do was look back to working at McDonald's, the Mac Shack, and I would understand again: "This is why I'm not going to quit." And people would always ask, "Why aren't you quitting?" "Ha! Cody, you're only making a tiny bit of money; you only made $10 on your first check." Or, "Cody, you have been doing that thing for a few months now. You're still working at McDonald's. You're still sign spinning. You're still doing school full-time, and you're not seeing any success." "Ha ha ha. You're never going to be successful, Cody." This was the typical conversation I had when people talked to me about my business.

I just thought, "OK. I'm not going to listen. I don't really care what these people have to say." I realized that network marketing turned into the best vehicle for me to get from where I was to where I wanted to be—regardless of what anyone said. Maybe this is something that can be a vehicle for you, but if not, this is my experience.

I knew this was the best vehicle for me ever since I was introduced to the industry earlier on in life and heard this acronym, which really stuck in my head—R-I-C-H, Residual Income Creates Happiness. It's the income that you create one time and continuously get paid on. I could have the freedom to do what I wanted, when I wanted, with whom I wanted, and however much I wanted. When I realized this was the way most wealthy people in the world created income, I was hooked. I definitely never thought I'd be where I am today. When I initially joined, I was 17, working two jobs, and a senior in high school getting mediocre grades, not showing much promise to my teachers.

When I first got started, there weren't any huge young success stories. I didn't really know what the heck I was going to do or if it was even possible. The system wasn't really set in place. There was a lot of trial and error, a lot of learning experiences—notice I didn't say failures; they are all learning experiences. Most of the people who joined me in my first six months were quitting. They were leaving as fast as they were coming in—it was a revolving door. But as I kept going, kept plugging away, I continued to learn more and more and more. I became addicted to the personal development and to learning more information. Most people quit because they can't see the long term in anything and just want instant gratification.

I believe the biggest game changer for me was when I was introduced to the movie, The Secret Movie: Law of Attraction. My entire life changed, literally overnight. I can credit almost 100 percent of my success in my life to seeing that movie and applying what I learned. I didn't watch it just one time; I watched it multiple times studying the information continuously. I watch it now once a month just to keep myself on the right track and thinking right. The way I think about things changed and continues to change. My mindset around what I needed to focus on became clearer; what I needed to do to become successful in all aspects of life became clearer. After watching the movie, my business literally doubled within a little over a month, just by making minor changes that compounded on themselves, just by thinking the right way, by focusing on the things I needed to focus on to get me where I wanted to go. By learning the "secret," I now get anything and everything I want—every time.

Instead of thinking, "I hope people show up to my event tonight." I say, "I know people are going to show up," and I get excited. Instead of "I hope these people get started," I say, "I know they're going to get started." I had 100 percent belief in where I was going and, being positive, focused on the things I wanted versus the things I didn't want. Bob Proctor says it best: "Talk about debt, whether it's good or bad debt, you are attracting debt. Talk about gaining more money and the abundance of money, and that's what you attract."

Things really seemed to be going great once I got this understanding down, and I was just about to graduate high school. I was ready to finish up and hit my business hard. That's when the unexpected hit me, right at the moment when things were going great. I developed the Epstein-Barr virus, Mono, otherwise known as the kissing disease, within literally a week of graduating high school and turning 18 years old.

Everyone was excited about going on graduation trips and stoked about their future, seeing that the world was right in their hands. I did get to enjoy a great trip to Hawaii with my family as I started getting sick. At the beginning, I didn't think it would be as bad as it was. I figured I could just fight through it. Coming off the tail end of the trip, I got extremely ill.

I was sick for a little over eight months. I was on bed rest, literally shut off from the outside world. I visited all sorts of doctors, got all kinds of injections, and had all kinds of procedures performed, checking out different parts of my body, checking to make sure everything was OK. I ended up in the hospital during one phase and literally experienced the worst day of my life. I was living in my parents' house at the time, and I was asleep in bed; I woke up and something didn't feel right at all—it really scared me. I felt as if I had just finished the hardest workout I had ever done, and my body was overexhausted. It was as if my body was in shock from something. I figured maybe I just needed to get a drink, so I rolled out of bed and started heading toward the kitchen.

As I struggled to walk, I couldn't help but drag my feet. I started looking around; my vision went really blurry, and my heart started beating really fast. I wasn't sure what was happening to me. I tried to get out to the living room to see if I could find one of my parents at home. I started shaking even more as I made it to the living room until I reached the point I could barely move, and I just fell down. I was very weak, and I wasn't sure what was happening. No one was home, and I literally thought I was going to die from some mysterious cause.

I called my parents. They weren't close enough to get there right away so I called 911 and had to be taken to the hospital. I honestly thought I was dying; I was unsure of what the future held. I was seeing spots and couldn't talk by the time the paramedics got me. I spent the rest of that day in the hospital wondering what was wrong with me. I started thinking about everything I still wanted to do in my life, to experience, and to see.

During that time, I was also thinking about everything I could have been doing, and I began getting really frustrated and feeling sorry for myself. I was at a really low point; I couldn't work on my business or exercise—the two things I had grown to love so much. To make matters worse, as I was continuing to recover I got some scary news from my grandmother. She called and said that Pop Joe had had a heart attack and was in the hospital. My family all flew to California to see him as he passed away. I was close with him; he supported me with everything I did, and I wanted him to see me succeed. It was at this point that I really began to feel hopeless. I spent a lot of frustrated nights at home crying because I couldn't enjoy life anymore.

I saw everyone else having so much fun. I would be on Facebook seeing everyone enjoying their lives and building the business I wanted to be building and me not being where I wanted to be. I was still barely able to get out of bed without becoming exhausted. Not only did it hurt my business during this eight-month period, it hurt me emotionally and mentally. I was drained. One of my biggest dreams had been to become a bodybuilder, which I had been training for up until the point I got sick and my body was in distress. Looking malnourished, unhealthy, and underweight, people definitely didn't forget to remind me how I looked.

When I was training for competition, I weighed over 170 pounds and had very low body fat. I was training, learning how to pose for competitions, and practicing every day. I was learning how to prep myself properly so I could go out there and compete to win. When I got sick, I lost all the progress I had worked for so hard every single day. I now struggled walking down the street without running out of energy. I dropped down to about 138 pounds once I was fully recovered. That's when everyone would say, "Cody, you're so skinny." "Cody, why do you look so unhealthy?" "Cody, why don't you eat more?" Or "Cody, why don't you work out?"

Things like that took a toll on my mental strength and my mental toughness; I was literally broken-hearted over it. It was a hard time in my life during which my business was taken away. My passion for bodybuilding was taken away. My health was taken away. Even my family had been taken away. I didn't know what to do; I was suffering from all these things and developed a condition called "brain fog."

Brain fog is a mental cloudiness which doctors aren't really sure how to fix. Picture that you're driving in the fog and you can't see clearly. That's how my head felt 24 hours a day. It was a really hard time and I didn't have much hope that I'd get where I wanted to be—I didn't know if I would ever recover. Even today, as I'm writing this book and building my business, there are still things that come up that are hard to do just because of that experience.

That experience caused emotions of depression and anxiety; I was not able to live up to the expectations I had for myself and to perform at a high level. Through all this, have still been able, now at 19, to create a great business and be surrounded by a great number of people. I don't tell many people about all these things I went through, but the truth is that things are going to happen to you in life, and you're going to get knocked down. There are going to be times when it looks like there's no hope, that there's no chance for you to keep moving forward, but you just have to. You just have to keep moving forward. I listened to Les Brown a lot while I was going through those hard times, and I remember he would always say, "Tough times have not come to stay; they have come to pass." I kept going and going, and thinking they would eventually pass if I just kept going.

I don't enjoy talking about those negative experiences because it brings back the memories. I feel I've had to talk about them because the people I looked up to when I wanted to succeed never showed any of the hardships they had to encounter on their way to the top. They don't talk about the negatives; they act like it's all sunshine and rainbows and happy days. Here is the wakeup call from me: Bad shit is going to happen. And when you think it is as bad as it can get, just know it can and will get better.

Obviously, it will be different for everybody; these are just some really hard things that happened to me. Once I broke through, I grew more as a person and got stronger. And during the time that I was sick, the one positive that I realized was the very real concept of residual income. I was getting paid every single week because I had built up an income in the business. I was getting paid continuously, and I didn't work for eight months.

I don't suggest direct sales or network marketing for everyone. I do, however, suggest creating some sort of residual secondary income. That was where I realized the power of what it could do; and, thinking back, that was something I needed. Think what would happen if something happened to you and you couldn't work for eight months. What would happen? What would your life look like if you didn't work anymore? Would everything be OK, or would it cause a lot of problems?

I still had bills to pay, and I still had income coming in, for which I was very blessed and grateful. This is the basis of my book. I'll show you that despite whatever you go through you can get to where you want to go. I will lay out the steps for you, the steps that I took, and the things that I learned from different network marketers, the things I've learned from different motivational speakers, from industry leaders, from the top CEOs of companies I've studied, from the things that have benefited me and got me to where I am today. Everything I've learned has helped me get to where I am. I basically lay out my experiences throughout my book; it is for you to take everything as you wish. If you like something, apply it to your life; if you don't, then don't. ■

CODY BARTON. *As a 20-year-old author and a top producer in a direct sales company, Cody Barton has developed a strong following of other young individuals interested in pursuing their dreams. Most young people do not have someone their own age that they can aspire to be like and to follow, and this leads some kids to end up doing something in their life that they don't really want to do. Cody has made it his mission to inspire other young people and those young at heart to pursue their dreams—no matter how big. Cody reached success by partnering with a couple of great mentors and accompanying this with an extreme work ethic. With those traits and a positive attitude he was able to accomplish what he is actually passionate about.*

Cody Barton
twitter - codybartonypr
instagram - codybartonypr
email- codybartonypr@gmail.com
website - Codybarton.com

Grieving is Deceiving
John Checki, Jr.

March 15, 1999: I lost my wife. At 6:00 a.m. (CST), I kissed my wife goodbye, and never saw her again. Luckily, I told her how much I loved her. She looked up at me—she was sleeping. That big long kiss of love woke her up, and it was too early in the morning for her to be anything but asleep, deep in happy dreams. "Are you okay?" She asked. "Yes, I'm fine." Wow! What a lucky break to have told her I loved her. Also, our home in Richardson, Texas, was foreclosed that same month. Yes, home foreclosure, lost wife, and a record earnings month—March, 1999, the Checki opera—something to cry about, and something to recover from.

March 15, 1999: At 2:35 p.m. (CST) on I-35, Janice Checki, my wife of nineteen years, lost control of our little station wagon, swerved off the highway down into a ditch, rolled over and over, per the police reports, then went airborne upside down over the southbound lanes of I-35. An off-duty EMT (Emergency Medical Technician) who had been riding his motorcycle in that southbound lane pulled over, turned off the ignition key to kill the engine, checked Janice for vital signs, and found none. She was gone from our lives.

She had left first thing in the morning; I was already at the office. She was on her way to see two of our kids down at Southwest Texas State University, along with our then only granddaughter, Ayla. It was a cool crisp day and a week full of appointments which did not get kept. She had left me a voice mail saying how she wished I was going with her. She had driven down to San Marcos many times, enjoyed the kids, and visited the outlet mall. Heck, we had both enjoyed the drive together in the past, not to mention the stop for kolaches at The Czech Stop—but that's another story.

That day did not go well, even before I knew what had happened in Budda, Texas. I just was not feeling well, so I went home. J.J., my college sophomore (or was he a junior?) was home from U.T. Austin for spring break—luckily he had decided not to accompany Janice down to San Marcos. Home, I had just fallen asleep, and the phone woke me right up. Chere, one of our friends down in San Marcos, was asking where Janice was. She was late. She did not have a cell phone, and, heck, if she did, it would not get answered; she would have a beer in one hand and a cigarette in the other—not sure how she steered and drove a stick shift. Yes, Janice drank and drove regularly, but not well.

As I was lying down after the call, I heard the unmistakable sound of a car driving up my front driveway, and a police radio—never a welcome experience. The front doorbell rang, and my son J.J. answered the door and was asked: "Are you John Checki?" He answered, "Yes." I quickly pulled on my jeans and went to the door as well.

"I'm John Checki."

"Are you married to Helen Janice Checki."

"Yes."

"You need to call the medical examiner's office in Austin."

"Is my wife deceased?"

"Do you need the number?"

I called down to Austin and was told the caseworker was out of the office, could I leave my name and number? Wow! I did not need that. I lay back down and took a deep, sickened breath. I got back up and picked up the phone. "Listen, I need to know if my wife, Helen Janice Checki, is deceased." "I can't tell you; the caseworker is out of the office." "Listen, I need to know. I will be happy to hold while you get permission from whomever you need to get permission to give me an answer."That was the longest, most tense and saddening hold on record.

"Hello?"

"Hi, this is John Checki, Helen Janice Checki's husband."

"Sir, your wife was involved in a high-speed car crash."

"Is she deceased?"

"Yes, sir. I am sorry to say she is gone. The investigating officer will get back to you."

"Thank you."

This will seem odd to you, but Janice and I had been married for nineteen years. We believe in heaven, hell, and Jesus. Death is a celebration of life, and the old things pass away, and we are face-to-face with the Lord. Still, I was one bawling mess inside. I called the Tissue Bank in Austin, and authorized them to reap whatever tissues and organs were salvageable, and dispose of her remains. They could take the tissue, I was told, but the remains were my responsibility. I hung up the phone. Suddenly I was single, and lost, confused, angry, hurt, abandoned, and….

How did I recover? And what is the rest of the story? And how will this help you? Well, first I called the kids and let them know mom did not make it. We cried, prayed, and wondered how the heck that had happened. Then I called family, starting with her father: "Hello, this is John Checki. I have some bad news."

"And?"

"Janice was killed in a car wreck this afternoon. Would you call Janet and Ben and let them know?"

"Yes. Thank you." Click. You guessed it—she and her dad were not close, especially since her mom, his wife, died. He remarried about nine months after her death—they had been married for almost fifty years. So it goes for widowers.

I called a couple of other people and quickly got tired of that. I asked Uncle Bill if he would call everyone else, and no, I had not yet decided where I would have the wake and funeral. I had a big drink of good, twelve-year-old Macallan Scotch. I opened the Bible to Ecceclesiates 3 to remind myself there is a time for all things, loving, living, and dying. It helped, but it also hurt. The phone rang: "Hi, this is Missy from the couples Bible study at Prestonwood Baptist. I was just calling to remind you and Janice about tonight."

"Ma'am, I do not mean to ruin your evening, but we won't make it to Bible study. Janice was killed in a car wreck this afternoon."

"Bless your heart."

"Thank you, Missy, I appreciate your call."

The doorbell rang. It was Bill and his good friend, John. "How are you holding up?"

"Well, I called the tissue bank in Austin, and the kids in San Marcos, and her dad. J.J. is here with me. How are y'all?"

"How are we? Are you kidding?"

"No, I'm not." They stayed awhile, then left. The doorbell rang again. It was one of the assistant pastors from Prestonwood. He did his best to comfort us, and we did our best to comfort him as well. (I know that sounds impossible.)

The rest of the week blurred on by with funeral arrangements, shipping of the remains, cleaning up the house to host the gathering after the funeral. One of the young ministers from Prestonwood would preside—he had never done a funeral. I wrote out the message: "Little Janice Is Gone." Yes, I used the occasion to throw in a biblical message and a "Come to Jesus" message. One of my Jewish clients came out of the service, gave me a hug and a smile and said, "Guess I'm going to Hell." Not the intent of the message, but, oh well.

Get to the point. How did I recover from being married all my adult life, comfort grieving almost-adult children and family, not to mention survive and thrive? A good friend, Chris, came by, and we had a drink and a nice long talk after the world of family left my home. He said he would be there for me, and I assured him I would be there for him as well. J.J. went back to U.T. down in Austin.

Honest to God, I gave a speech one week to the day later for the Rotary Club in McKinney ("How to have fun and still have $$.") The first

Sunday after Janice died, I went to the Zig Ziglar Encouragers Class at Prestonwood. I was walking through jello. I was invited to give my testimony and declined—I didn't want to be identified as a widower with a target on his forehead for silly single women searching for a fully trained husband now suddenly single. I went to the Dallas Opera as well—don't ask me which one. How did I recover? Well, I spent a lot of time at the gym working out—we are talking most afternoons, most of the afternoon—long walks morning and evening, as well as lots of Blue Bell ice cream. Within three weeks of the funeral, my office phone began to ring. Single ladies who had known us had suddenly developed a need for financial planning now that Janice was dead. I had been warned about this. The calls did not get returned.

I continued working out, going to church, making the speeches which I had committed to make, and I saw clients ten days after Janice died. Oddly, they had called another client in town, Jed, and asked if he thought I would be there. Jed laughed and said: "If John says he will be there, he will be there and prepared; that is just the way he is." And I was. I'm not sure that would work for everyone, but if I have something to do, and I have a passion for it, it will get done or I will die trying to get it done—Are we clear on this?

Recovery

The days were filled with the blur of long, hard workouts, client meetings, writing "PopUps" daily, counseling, grief recovery classes, and church-related recovery meetings, lost keys, a misplaced car, a gym locker break-in, and more phone calls from single women who had attended the funeral. Then the phone rang, and a friend wanted to have dinner together; she asked, "Would I?" Lynn was a fellow speaker/writer and friend, "Sure." Just to make life as complete as it could be, the night of our dinner was the Columbine massacre. Lynn was a news consultant and glued to the television. Man, if this is dating, include me out. Eventually, she turned off the set, we had dinner, and I started telling stories of growing up in Jersey, playing tag with the taxis along Fifth Avenue. There's nothing like driving an MG down Fifth to the Village and then parking in a bus stop—not sure how my car did not get towed.

I continued with scuba diving stories from when I was only fourteen and learned how to dive at the YMCA in downtown Hackensack; bought a tank, regulator, and the rest of the gear, took another course and went diving; joined the Sea Scouts and sailed to Long Island; played tag with the ocean liners in a sixteen-foot MFG fiberglass runabout powered by a seventy-five horsepower motor; thumbed through a catalogue of colleges and ran across T.C.U. and applied—something about more girls than boys, and I have always liked girls more than boys; they had a football team, were moderately selective, had reasonable tuition and room and board and books, and were far away from New Jersey. She told me I was a great storyteller, and I thought this must be dating—your jokes are funny and everyone wants a ride in your convertible. We parted the same way we started, as friends, or kissing cousins, I forget which.

More recovery, more dates, the first "here is my key why don't you come over for dinner later tonight." Wow, had dating changed since 1969! The dinner was quick and the evening led to sunrise and breakfast. I enrolled in The Comedy Gym, signed up for the wrong list and went up on stage and died in public for the first time. The recovery continued for an intense week —then it was Thanksgiving. I had invited the kids; we had a problem over them going to a particular liquor store which had supplied Janice with way too many cases of beer. We kissed and made up and had a nice dinner. I went to South Beach, Florida, the next day for a Blackbeard Live Aboard diving cruise.

South Beach lived up to all the hype—great beach, lots of bars, a neat little hotel, and a total absence of taxis. I caught a limo—No kidding!—a limo which had just dropped off four cigar-smoking guys. I was standing outside the hotel. I had dive gear all around me. The limo driver/owner asked if I needed a ride. "Yes." We had a great talk about South Beach, the limo business, life in general, and why everyone was taking pictures of a particular mansion. That much-photographed home turned out to be the recently murdered designer Versace's mansion. Oh!

Blackbeard Cruises used former Sea Scout boats; these were little sailing cruisers which drifted all over the place when they were kind enough to let me steer for a short while. I enjoyed my dives, but not the saltwater showers. The other guests were all from Southern California. For eleven days we went anywhere from Miami to Bimini, Nassau, and many little cays which I could not begin to remember. I caught a cold at the end of the trip and missed two days of dives rather than risk popping an ear drum.

I caught that same limo driver back to the airport—this time he brought me a stretch limo. It was nice and memorable to ride in style in Miami for once. The flight home was uneventful. The days that followed were not. It was the Christmas season, the first single Christmas I had had since I was twenty years old, and now I was fifty-one and turning fifty-two in a month. Lots of singles class events. Let me tell you, the only difference between a country-and-western bar and a singles class at a large church is there is no two-drink minimum at the church—but there is lots of lust and bust going on. I had never even imagined this is the way single life would be other than reading *Playboy Magazine* a million years ago. Again, life had changed a great deal since then—Beware of the Ides of March! I did stand-up comedy and discovered I was better at marketing the event, putting butts in the seats than I was at telling jokes. But I did get laughs and entertain; and I learned how not to step on the laughs.

There were side effects of this single-widower life, I was so popular on Match.com that I was interviewed by the *Dallas Morning News*. They then followed me around on a made-for-the-newspaper-date. Now I know why celebrities disdain the paparazzi. Nothing's quite as silly as being followed around in public by a bazooka-size lens and popping flashbulbs. Ginger and I went to a comedy club, and disrupted the place—sorry about that—but it was a while back, and no one got famous in between time, and Ginger is now married (not to me) and a mom.

What was the biggest funny challenge to recovering? Learning to say "me" instead of "us," and not putting six pounds of chicken or a rack of butterfly pork chops on the grill—who the heck did I think I was cooking for? And did I forget to tell myself who I had invited over? No, but luckily I had a big freezer. Also the distraction of dating rather than being married cost me time and energy, despite getting to date half of north central Texas for two full years. What were the other costs? My financial planning practice suffered. I had the worst year in ten years, 2000. In 1999, I lost the house, my wife, and my focus. Six months into 2001, I was back up and running well. In 1999 and 2000, I had two of everything—keys, rings, notebooks, calculators, appointment books, and my marbles were misplaced and replaced regularly.

Solutions

What is life like now? And how could you benefit from this?

After the spiral of losing my wife, experiencing a home foreclosure, having a terrible year financially, and having my family torn apart from grief and moving, what were the solutions?

1. Putting some stability back in my financial life by focusing on my financial planning practice like never before.
2. Attending widowed persons' services events.
3. Going to the Italian Club of Dallas and meeting my gorgeous and talented wife, Suzi.
4. In time, taking on a continuity partner for my practice.
5. Training my son, J.J. Checki, III, as a registered office assistant.
6. Getting plenty of good coaching and counseling.
7. The support of family, friends, and clients.
8. Moving our home and my office.
9. Writing about it.
10. Giving speeches about it.
11. Returning to Paris and Rome for vacation, and adding Venice and Florence to the trip.
12. Adding perspective to my life.
13. Learning how to dance, sing, and do stand-up comedy.
14. Getting rid of things that did not work and replacing them with things that do.
15. Passing on the following:

a) Get help from professionals and from fellow widows or widowers, family, and friends;
b) get fit and healthy;
c) offer service to others;
d) write, laugh, dance, cook more, eat out less, and
e) love—yes, most importantly, give love and be loved. ▪

 JOHN CHECKI, JR. *lists as his accomplishments his training: CPA (Certified Public Accountant), CFP® (Certified Financial Planner), CRC® (Certified Retirement Counselor), and his education: B.A. in economics, T.C.U., B.B.A. in accounting, U.T.A. John writes: The best part of life has been: husband to the gorgeous and talented Suzi Checki, father to Stephanie Checki-Alexander, and J.J. Checki, III, grandfather (Pop) to Lil Kory, Cameron, Sarah, Elizabeth, and Zachariah. Financial advisor to clients for the past twenty-five years, many of John's clients have been with him that entire time. John was in the Army, is a black belt in TKD, went to several stand-up comedy schools, and has done stand-up. "From Here and Now to WOW"® is Mr. Checki's registered trademark. He writes: "It's how I do my best to help clients."*

John Checki, Jr.
www.johncheckijr.com
972-437-4089,
2435 North Central Expressway,
Suite 1508,
Richardson, TX 75080

4

The Trust Factor
Shahidrah Cowgill

I n his grace, God has given us different gifts for doing certain things well. So if God has given you the ability to prophesy, speak out with as much faith as God has given you (See Romans 12:6).

In my field, I am blessed to have the opportunity to work with everyday people who contend with life challenges. Whenever counseling services are initiated for an individual, teen, or family, I expect to answer many questions about the counseling process and any clinically relevant information about myself. To establish a healthy rapport with my clients, each individual is offered an opportunity to ask me any question they may have about therapy. Oftentimes, teens will ask personal questions like, "You got any kids?" or "Do you like cats?" But most often I am asked, "How did you get that scar?" For someone to inquire about a scar, it must be visible. All of us have scars and wounds that we carry from life experiences. Our scars, be they physical, emotional, relational, visible, or invisible, have a story attached, and mine are no different.

Our stories of hope, faith, redemption, restoration, healing, and deliverance are meant to be shared because it encourages the soul and spirit of others. We all struggle and have life challenges but we are not meant to stay in that low place. God's wellness plan for each of our lives is for us to live in health, fulfill our purposes, and prosper (See 3 John 1:2). So if God wants us to have healthy relationships and the best life possible, why does He allow us to be wounded? Many people struggle with this concept and, consequently, can't see past themselves and their pain. But it is in the suffering that our lives are changed. We each have a choice to either find value in the lessons that are taught during that season or stay stuck reliving, rehashing, and reopening old wounds. A sign of maturity and growth is not in the reporting of how tough our life has been but it is in our willingness to share transparently how we made it through.

My Story

In January 2012, my maternity leave was coming to an end. I was a new mom with a boutique private practice and a full-time job to which I seriously questioned whether it was worth it for me to return. It was a difficult decision for me to go back but, with my husband's urging, I'm grateful that I did. In hindsight, I now know that my purpose for being back to work for just one month before I got laid off was for an encounter with an angel on my last day as an employee.

That day in February went by fast and, just as I was preparing to leave, I ran into a co-worker named Angela who I had not seen the entire month that I had been back to work. After she welcomed me back and asked how my baby was doing she said, "What's that on your neck?" I replied, "I don't know, is it a scratch?" I did have a new baby after all; a scratch would have been expected.

She looked more intently and said, "No, that is not a scratch; it looks like a lump." Those are words nobody wants to hear. She had no clue that during that time my father-in-law was in the throes of cancer treatment, and I had a front-row seat to the reality of loss, sickness, and death. The outcome of what a "lump" meant was very frightening to me. She took me to the bathroom and showed me in the mirror what she saw. She said, "I don't want to scare you. The only reason I noticed it was because I had something similar. I had a goiter on my thyroid, and it needed to be removed because it was blocking my airway." She encouraged me to go get it checked out and removed.

Needless to say, getting furloughed and navigating this work-life transition was no longer at the top of my list of concerns. I called my doctor that same day. Maybe there was a reason all of this was happening now—I really didn't know. What seemed like just a transitional phase for work was shaping up to be more than what my natural eyes could see.

The next day I had an appointment with my family doctor. My husband came along just in case there was bad news—I didn't want to be given it alone. The doctor greeted us, asked a few questions, and said, "Well, let me take a look at you." And then she simply said, "Yep! That's a goiter. You are the third patient with an enlarged thyroid that I have seen this week." She explained it was a fairly common condition in postpartum women, and rarely was it anything that required aggressive treatment. However, she still checked my thyroid levels, sent me for an ultrasound and biopsy, and referred me to an ENT specialist. Both of us left that appointment with a mild sense of relief.

A few days later, I visited the ENT and learned that my thyroid levels were normal and the ultrasound and biopsy report came back stating that the lump was benign—NOT cancerous. My ENT made me aware of all my options, removal surgery being the most aggressive. At that time, I decided that since it was not cancerous I wanted to follow up with her in six months to have it checked again, which was the least invasive option. She said, "Most of the time, these things aren't harmful or cancerous, so let's just watch it and see if it continues to grow." I felt like I had dodged a bullet and that I could get back to living life, building my practice, and raising my new family.

As spring arrived, I set some personal goals to balance my health and well-being in all areas. Along with following up with doctor appointments, exercising, eating right, getting good sleep, and valuing my relationships, I had also started attending a noon prayer group every week at my church. It was something that I wanted and needed to do to get closer to God, nurture my faith, and connect with other believers.

While busy trying to do a better job of taking care of myself, I had an annual appointment with my OBGYN. My doctor touched my neck and gave a puzzled look. Before she could speak, I cut the silence with, "It has already been checked out. I have had an ultrasound and a biopsy, and I met with an ENT too. It is no big deal."

She responded, "Well, that's good. So, why is it still in there?"

I stammered with the answer that my ENT and family doctor gave me, "We are just watching it."

She looked at me and boldly said, "For what? You are still young. It's just going to get bigger, and you can't take it out when you are pregnant. They don't ever know 100 percent what it is until it is out. GET IT TAKEN OUT." Dr. Holt pointed to a faint scar on her neckline and said, "I had mine removed; trust me, it is better out than in."

When God sends a message that He wants you to get, He keeps sending His messengers. God was definitely trying to get my attention. So instead of me continuing with my "no big deal attitude," I went to prayer group.

The Purpose and Benefits of Prayer

At my point of need, I knew that I had to do something different. My old way of doing things was not working. I thought I had done what I could do by trusting those who were on my medical care team to give me their best suggestions, but I was still missing the bigger message. I had chosen to be passive, waiting for more physical evidence so I could make a difficult decision. My soul was not at peace; the truth is, I was very afraid of surgery and all of the "what ifs" that came along with it.

Prayer allowed me time to get still enough to humble myself so that I could hear God's voice. In that time, I realized that instead of fully trusting God to be in control, I was holding on to fear and not exercising my faith (see Proverbs 3:5). God was waiting for me to release ALL things to Him.

There are many benefits to prayer that have been highlighted in secular research and founded on biblical principles. Here are a few perks. Adding prayer to your self-care plan:

1. Relieves stress and reduces stress related disorders.

2. Opens us up to hope and increases our measure of faith.
3. Allows us to experience God's divine help and intervention.
4. Offers clarity, direction, and strength for daily decision-making and during difficult situations.
5. Is linked to greater emotional and physical health, as well as the strengthening of the immune system.

After only three months, I scheduled to meet with my ENT and told her that I wanted to move forward with the surgery. The ENT shared that she had not seen any change but whole-heartedly supported my decision to have it removed.

On August 23rd, everything went according to plan. The doctor conducted the partial thyroidectomy. I spent a couple of days in the hospital recovering and was well on my way to healing. I could not talk; however, I was able to tolerate eating a little food and swallowing liquids, and all my vital signs were good. I needed to rest and that was my job for the next couple of weeks—doctor's orders.

Five days into recovery I got a follow-up phone call from my ENT doctor. She said, "Shahidrah, your pathology report has come back, and the pathologist found some cancer, a rare form that is hard to detect. I am sorry to have to share this with you over the phone. We typically would have you come in to receive news such as this; however, it is an urgent matter." She further recommended that I have the other side of my thyroid removed. "We have already reserved a spot for you in the next couple of days to have the second surgery; all we need is your yes to move forward."

She then said, "Good thing you chose to get it out when you did; had you waited any longer to do this it could have possibly spread to other parts of your body."

The Victory

My entire thyroid was removed in the summer of 2012. I still had to submit to the process of removing what was causing me harm, something that I could not initially see with my own eyes. I went through an extended recovery period of six months with a paralyzed vocal cord and whisper tone of a voice. In 2014, there is no sign of cancer in my body, and I am fully restored. My scar is a representation of my testimony of God's healing power.

1. We need God. His order and timing are perfect. He knows what we need before we know we have a need. Through prayer He offers us access to peace, healing, love, joy, acceptance, forgiveness, divine intervention, and much more when we are obedient and connected to Him.

2. Your health and wellness are important. Spiritual balance and faith are necessary components for living a healthy life.

3. We need each other. Whatever you go through, the lesson is not just for you. Had Angela and Dr. Holt not walked in their purpose, I would not have gotten the message I needed that saved my life. It's never just about you. If you miss the lesson, you miss the message that you need to pay forward. Your scar story may hold the key to somebody else's breakthrough. ■

48

SHAHIDRAH COWGILL. *A licensed psychotherapist, Shahidrah Cowgill is the owner of Fundamental Foundations Counseling in Frisco, Texas. She has several years of clinical experience in the mental health field providing outpatient counseling and psychotherapy services to children, adolescents, adults, couples, and families with complex mental health and relationship issues. Shahidrah specializes in helping those who may feel overwhelmed with life's struggles find a healthy balance caring for themselves and for their family relationships so they can live fulfilling and meaningful lives. In 2013, she founded and launched BeAHealthyParent.com, an online resource for parents and caregivers of young children. She offers research-inspired, spiritually based, practical tools to help address and improve relational, behavioral, and developmental struggles parents may face with their children. Classes, video lessons, consultations, and supportive community Q&A calls provide convenient access to information and application strategies that may help decrease parenting, childhood-behavior, and family issues before they become an overwhelming problem. Shahidrah is a consultant, speaker, trainer, and advocate in the early childhood field. She is passionate about strengthening families and empowering parents so that our communities and society become better, healthier, and safer.*

Shahidrah Cowgill, M.A., LPC, NCC
Fundamental Foundations Counseling
9191 Kyser Way Ste. 200
Frisco, TX 75033
www.FriscoPsychotherapist.com
214-475-0345
Be A Healthy Parent
www.BeAHealthyParent.com
877-269-5946

5

"DBA: Decide Believe Act"
Tracy D. Day

L et us think for a moment about the title of this book, *Dare to be a Difference Maker*. What does that really mean to you? You may be thinking, "How can I be a difference maker?" Or perhaps, "I am not famous enough or worthy to make a difference."

I am here to tell you that you are worthy, and that you can make a difference! To make a difference is simply to have an impact. Everyone on the planet makes a difference to someone. Some differences are small things, such as opening a door for someone or giving up your seat in a crowded room. You might be making a difference by volunteering for an organization that has had an impact on your life or on someone you know.

Regretfully, not all impacts are positive. What if a mother was on illegal drugs while she was pregnant? Our society today would curse her yet have sympathy for the baby. I was that baby. I was born addicted. I came into this world on time, a "strong" five pounds and seven ounces, and thirteen inches tall. I jokingly tell others I was no bigger than my shoe size. The doctors stated that my eye sight was limited and I might go blind. Some would say I had little or no chance of survival or of being a productive member of society.

The state immediately put me in foster care. However, I had someone who made a difference in my life. My foster parents, who eventually became my mom and dad, gave me love, hope, and a sense of belonging.

I owe my life to Vernon and LaNita Day. My strength to grow and become stronger came from them. I learned how to be a difference maker through the actions of my parents. They made a difference to everyone in our small community, in our state, and even on a national level.

My dad served 35 years full-time in the Texas Army National Guard. As I was growing up, it seemed that everyone in town worked with or for him one weekend a month and two weeks during the year. I could not go anywhere without someone telling me, and usually matter-of-factly, "Do I need to call your daddy?" The old saying "It takes a village to raise a child" was true for those of us who grew up in our small town. Everyone knew everybody, and we all made a difference to each other. My mom showed me it is never too late to make a difference. After raising four boys, she obtained her nursing degree and enlisted as an officer in the military with my dad. One of my proudest moments was my mom giving me my last oath while serving in the military. My life as a child and as an adult was made possible by them. They made a HUGE difference in my life.

As I grew older, a schoolmate and friend's dad was always around providing encouragement to each one of us in our own special way. No matter the environment, no matter the situation, he always had the right words to uplift us. Eventually, he became the little league baseball coach for the team I played for. He often called upon me to pitch during practice and against the toughest teams. He would push me to my limits even though he knew I was struggling. My arm was tired, our team was getting beat, and my mental game was suffering, but he continued to encourage each of us. I found myself mocking his words to me, "Rock 'n fire, Tracy. Rock 'n fire. You can do it, Preserver!"

I never really understood the true meaning behind that until years later. I realized he was telling me to hang in there, that I can do it. I can overcome my obstacle and win. To this day, I can still hear his voice when life is scoring on me and I am down a few runs. I muster the strength to stand tall, head up, and attack the day with confidence—and make a difference to those around me.

It didn't take long for me to truly understand what he meant by "Preserver." A few years after completing little league baseball, I was helping my old coach work with the new kids coming into the game. We knew we were going to have a great team and be one of the top contenders for the title. It was my opportunity to give back to them what had been given to me.

I was in a good place in my life in high school and all was well for me as a small-town teenager. Draft day came and one of the parents who was to coach a team backed out—on draft day! Really? The impact of losing a team was detrimental to the schedule and to the 12–15 kids on that team. How was this going to be resolved? I made a choice to make a difference. I didn't realize at the time, but my attitude was to be a servant leader like my dad and my coach. The league president and other coaches agreed to let me coach, but they would be watching me.

Watch they did, all the way to the championship game. Here I was, coaching in the championship game, as the student, in a fierce battle against my former coach, the teacher. I was facing the very team I was to help coach at the beginning of the year. We lost in a close game, but the true winners were those kids on my team. I made a difference in their lives. One of those kids went on to be an outstanding running back as a high school senior, and many of them have gone on to successful careers as adults. There are times when I travel back to my hometown where those kids live now as adults, and I am reminded of that great summer when I was their coach. I made a difference.

I hope as you read this that I am encouraging you to make a positive difference in your world. It starts with three things. First, DECIDE that you want to make a difference. You have great things in you. You can make a difference to your own children, your friends, your co-workers—even people you don't know. I honestly trust and believe the adage: "What goes around comes around." Our world is a fast-paced rat race. Everyone seems to want something for him or herself, and rarely does anyone take the time to uplift someone around them. Take a moment to brighten another person's day.

This reminds me of two friends who care for one another. Life had

52

taken them on their separate paths, but the two stayed in contact. They decided to reconnect and catch up on life's events. The man gave his friend a pair of earrings since she enjoyed wearing and collecting earrings. I understand that to this day she still has them. It was a small gesture, but it was authentic. It made a difference in her life. She knew that he cared for her. I challenge you to stand out of the crowd and be a positive light to brighten another's day. I believe you can do it.

This leads into the second factor, BELIEVE in your decision to be a difference maker. I wake up every day with a positive attitude, thinking about how wonderful my day will be and how I will make a difference in my own way. I may not save the world or find a cure for a disease, but I do believe that I will make a difference to someone that day. I have no idea what I will do or to whom I will make a difference, but I know I will.

I challenge you to open a door for someone, give up your seat, smile, ask another person how their day is going. I encourage you to put something positive into their bucket. "Attitude is everything," as some people say. I would agree to a point, but if it were all about attitude I would be the wealthiest person in the world. Attitude is not everything, but it is one thing that can make a difference in your life for you to be a difference maker to those around you. Your attitude and belief are valuable assets on your journey to being that difference maker.

The third factor is to ACT on your decision and belief. Act and conduct yourself like the leader you are or want to become. A mirror reflects a man's face, but who he really is shows in his actions. This is a simple but true fact of life. As you grow into being a difference maker, your friends will change. Mine did, and that is OK. The less you associate with some people, the more your life will improve. The more you tolerate mediocrity in others, the more it increases your mediocrity.

I have learned through leaders with whom I have associated and who have mentored me that they all have this one attribute: being impatient with negative-thinking and negative-acting people. As you grow and make that positive difference, your thought process, your actions, and your associates will change. Wise is the person who fortifies his life with the right friendships. Work hard to turn ideas into innovations that improve lives or turn the ordinary into the extraordinary. What you do makes a difference. What you do moves the world forward.

A couple desired to improve their situation and to restart their lives across the country. They knew it was going to be tough and they called upon friends for support. And the friends they contacted agreed to help them. The couple then acted on their decision and belief that life could be better, and they moved their young, new family across the country. It was a tough time, but they had the right attitude of success. They had support from their friends that success was on the way. And success has come for that couple. They both are successful in their respective careers, and their oldest child is beginning his own successful life in college. Collectively, their attitudes and belief that their efforts would make a difference were invaluable to their success. The support from their friends proved to make a difference in their own way.

Tom Brokaw once said, "It's easy to make a buck. It's a lot tougher to make a difference." I do not think it is tough; it just may be some time before you see results, but your effort will make a difference, which is the important thing. Be a person of encouragement, like my little league coach. Be a person with whom others want to associate. There is a saying, "If you run with wolves, you will learn how to howl. However, if you associate with eagles you will learn to soar to great heights." Decide, believe, and act to be a positive difference maker to those around you.

You may think that the only way to make a change is to work with those at the top. The important task of making a difference is achieved by helping others move forward with clarity and confidence, even if they face setbacks. As your leadership skills develop, continue to build a solid foundation for your interactions with others. You can foster trust and inspire confidence by acting in a reliable manner. In short, it may be tough, but I believe that we can all be an example for others to follow.

We live in a very fast-paced world; however, we all make time for what is important to us. I find that it only takes a moment to make a difference. You can do that! Spare a moment to make a difference. We all can do that. It starts with a small gesture of kindness. That gesture will grow into a habit and eventually become a part of who you are as an individual.

I served in the military like my dad and mom, and I gained valuable leadership skills. Along the way, through reading books and having great mentors, I developed great people skills and built a desire to share the greatness that has been bestowed in me. I feel that it is now my responsibility to pass along those developed skills to others. I decided, believed, and acted on my desire to become a Zig Ziglar Legacy Certified speaker and coach. I spent a powerful week with some of the most amazing business owners and professionals. Initially, being among such amazing individuals, I felt out of place, but, once I realized the greatness in me and the gift I was given to make a difference, I knew I belonged. The best part of the entire process is that we each want to make a difference in someone's life.

We have all heard the saying, "If he can do it, I can do it." I believe deep down this is true. The human mind is a powerful force in the universe. Once your mind is made up, give yourself permission to truly make a difference to others, and know you can do it. Speak with your spouse or close friend and inform them of your decision—and get support from them. On your journey to make a difference, create a compelling future, uplift those who need assistance along the way, and give people credit and recognition for actions that demonstrate positive values and principles.

Remember, you can make a difference. You can be a positive impact to everyone around you. I know after reading this book you will feel empowered to be the best you can be. The great Ralph Waldo Emerson said: "To leave the world a bit better…to know that one life has breathed easier because you have lived. This is to have succeeded." Once you are successfully applying your version of "Dare to Make a Difference," keep applying your ideas and principles. The way to remain great is to make a difference, impact someone's life, and keep making those around you better than good and greater than great! ■

TRACY D. DAY, *CEO/President of Tracy Day Motivation in San Antonio, Texas, has worked in the information technology profession for over 28 years. As an infant, Tracy was adopted into a military household. Growing up in a military family and experiencing leadership throughout his young life, Tracy began his career in the United States Air Force and served nearly 14 years. Currently, he serves as an IT consultant for the United States Air Force.*

Tracy is a Wayland Baptist University graduate. He received his bachelor's in Information Systems Management. Tracy holds a variety of technical certifications in the IT field. He also owns a financial services business and is currently licensed at the state and federal levels.

He has been involved in various leadership roles throughout his career. While in the Air Force, Tracy held the role of Local Area Network Manager. As a consultant, he was hand-selected to lead a team of individuals for a national project that covered the country coast to coast, including Alaska. He currently serves in a role that works closely with Microsoft and other federal agencies and impacts millions. Tracy has presented and spoken at a number of technical conferences and to senior management in a variety of organizations.

In Tracy's burgeoning financial services career, he has been called upon to conduct training with small organizations in his local area. Tracy was hand-selected by the Ziglar Corporation to be among the first 40 Ziglar Legacy Certified trainers and speakers in the world. Tracy speaks on building winning relationships, goal setting and achievement, building a better you, and other leadership principles.

Being adopted into a loving family changed his life to the tune of having a good-natured, fun-loving attitude. He demonstrates that same attitude with his wife and three children. Tracy's approach and belief is to have a positive impact on everyone he meets and to make a difference in their life.

Tracy Day
Tracy@TracyDayMotivation.com
www.tracydaymotivation.com

Turning Despair into Dreams
Shauna Ekstrom

Before you can help others to change, you have to first experience change for yourself.

I've always marched to the beat of a different drummer. Perhaps that's what eventually led me to start my career path and family much earlier than most. I quit high school at fifteen, graduated from cosmetology school and married by seventeen, and had my first child at eighteen. You could say that I was in a hurry to be an adult. I looked like a grown woman with my big hair and make-up, but I saw the world through the inexperienced eyes of a teenager. However, I absolutely loved being a mom. But this inexperience of the real world and not knowing that everything can't be fixed by going shopping kept us on the never-ending financial stress wheel.

Just like a lot of families, we always seemed to have too much month at the end of the money. It was not all doom and gloom, however, because I could go CREATE every day in my hair salon. To me, hair styling is an art form, and I was passionate about the creative side of hair. Every day someone new would walk into my salon, and I would be given the opportunity not only to help them look beautiful on the outside but to also feel better about themselves on the inside. I have always felt that "natural" is way overrated. We had a win/win situation in that I felt great when I saw the wonderful change in my clients' confidence and self-esteem, and they felt confident enough to reach inside and let others see their inner beauty.

If you are a hair stylist, aesthetician, personal trainer, life coach, teacher, or caring friend, never underestimate the positive impact on someone that a little change here and there can make. Beauty can be bought and taught. It was through my daily interaction with my hair salon clients and my children that my passion for understanding people and psychology started.

Not all change has to be earth-shattering or stressful. Sometimes, all it takes is for someone to listen and care, or for another person to say they believe in you. I loved my hair styling career; it was creative and there was something new every day. But mostly I loved making a positive difference in people's lives. Making men and women feel understood, prettier, and giving them a place to come where someone really listened was heartwarming.

I was a hair stylist for over thirty-four years total, and my last hair salon was a small private boutique studio called **The Red Door Salon**. It was in a quaint small town named Enumclaw, Washington, nestled at the base of Mount Rainier. It was here that a few years earlier my friend Joni introduced me to network marketing. Prior to reluctantly attending my first meeting with Joni, I was totally ignorant of the profession and believed that it was one big rip off. I had always shied away from it because, rather than do my own research, I listened to the warnings of others who were probably as unknowledgeable as I was tell me that it was a scam or that it just didn't work. As it turned out, the most expensive thing I'd ever owned, until then, was a closed mind.

However, it was during our first meeting that I experienced an epiphany. I was in a room filled with people who were excited about life, hungry for more, and going for their dreams. I WAS EXCITED!!! Experiencing this made me realize that I could do it too. I had found my way out of despair and financial misery. In this moment, I was not just interested in doing what was convenient, I was committed to doing whatever it took to change my life. It was going to take a few years, but it was my way out.

My second epiphany came a few weeks later at the company meeting when I heard a speaker say:

Make you strengths productive and your weaknesses irrelevant.

This blew my mind. I had no doubts about the network marketing industry, but I did have some doubts about my ability to make it work. However, as soon as I understood that all I had to do was make my strengths even stronger, I was up and running.

Like I said, sometimes just a few words can change someone's life. I had found a way to get off the financial stress wheel; and now I had a belief that made it possible for me to dream and hope. This is a powerful combination. My family and I now had a future with options.

A man devoid of hope and conscious of being so has ceased to belong to the future.

—Albert Camus (Algerian-born French author, philosopher, and journalist, awarded the Nobel Prize for Literature in 1957, the youngest ever to receive the reward)

I was not an overnight success, but I was empowered by hope and my dreams. I studied the industry; I focused on learning all I could on personal development; and I worked diligently. At the start, it was difficult. Because I didn't know what I was doing, I just did what the top achievers told me to do. It never felt quite right, but I was a newbie so I thought it was just me. Five companies and fifteen years later, however, I can tell you that my gut was right. I eventually stopped listening to everyone and started to listen to myself. As soon as I did this, my network marketing career changed for the better. With every little success I became more confident of my different approach to network marketing, and ultimately developed my"Heartfelt Network Marketing Manifesto."

I have always come from the position of genuinely wanting to help people to feel better about themselves and to give them hope for the future. I found that network marketing was a very doable thing, and would help me do just that. Building my network marketing business on a part-time basis while still running my salon gave me so much hope.

The principles of Heartfelt Network Marketing have allowed me to dramatically change, both physically and financially, my life, my family's life, and the lives of tens of thousands of people across the country.

I sold my shop in 2006 because my passion for making a difference in people's lives and providing them with a space where they felt understood and heard had taken a different turn. I always believed that I was making a difference in people's lives; however, I was very aware that it was only for a short time, that maybe it would last six to eight weeks until their next hair appointment. I wanted to focus on helping people make lifetime changes. I am talking about a legacy that will affect future generations.

I transitioned to a full-time professional Heartfelt Network Marketer and within a couple of years I hit the famous six-figure income bracket— and now I am in the millionaire category. Not bad for a girl who started as a teenage mom, was a high school dropout, and had a passion for shopping on a miner's wages.

I still get to meet new people every day; however, through my business network organization, which at the writing of this book is in excess of 110,000 people, we get to help hundreds each day.

It isn't complicated. Many people are drowning in despair and hopelessness due to their never-ending problem of continually running out of time and money. The stress of this alone can kill you, not to mention the effect it has on your long term health . These people go through each day feeling that there is nothing they can do to change their future; all hope has gone, and their dreams have turned to dust, so they don't even try. I have come across this scenario time and time again. My role is to listen and understand what is going on in a person's life, and, if appropriate, I will respectfully ask permission to tell them my personal story. Often, just knowing that I don't have a college degree and that I really did start out in life on the wrong side of the tracks gives them hope that maybe, just maybe, they too can break free of their daily financial stress.

Had I not gone against the norm when I was a young girl, I'm sure that I would have never discovered my current career. This incredible career has changed the lives of my children, my grandchildren, and tens of thousands of people who I have been able to touch both directly and indirectly because of my story and by sharing what I consider a gift; Network Marketing the heartfelt way.

I am a Heartfelt Network Marketer and I am proud of it. Why wouldn't I be? It is an honorable profession which affords me the time and money to help people physically and emotionally. It is through this profession that I was able to save my eldest son's life when he nearly died from an addiction that was bigger than him. I had the money to keep him in rehab for as long as he needed to fully recover; and today I am proud to say that he is alive and well, has a fantastic career, and is giving hope to others with similar challenges. My daughter, Heidi Poche, who also has written a chapter in this book, has the time and financial freedom because she said yes to network marketing. She's able to have a fantastic and fulfilling career at home, raising my three adorable grand-daughters. I have also been able to buy my mother a home that she enjoys, and put my youngest son through university so that he graduated without any student loans. I also enjoy supporting charities that help other less fortunate people.

It is time the stigma is lifted from network marketing and people are given a chance to explore the opportunities without prejudice. My goal is to help raise the bar of the profession and, in doing so, help many more individuals, single parents, and families struggling through life to see that there are options. There are alternatives to a lack of time, money, and fun. This profession has a great deal to offer, not the least of which is the opportunity to meet and mix with people who are focused on personal growth and realizing their dreams

I know what it is like to be on the outside looking in. I used to want to fit in so badly that I would go on shopping sprees and buy stylish clothes so that our family looked like everyone else's—all the time knowing that we didn't have the money to pay the credit card bills at the end of the month. I used to be so scared about the bills that I would hide the unopened envelopes in a box, hoping they would magically disappear. Thanks to the personal development training and the great speakers and top achievers I have met in the network marketing profession, I learned that I didn't need to change to fit in, I just needed to find a group of friends and colleagues who were like me.

The network marketing profession is overflowing with caring, hard-working, motivated, fun, supportive individuals who started with nothing and then found hope and started to dream. I am one of them, and I am proof that it can be done without compromising your ethics and alienating your family and friends—although through my excitement over my new-found freedom, I did in the beginning. Mixing with like-minded people takes all the stress out of being you.

I don't resent starting out with two strikes against me because it gave me a chance to learn a very important lesson:

"If it is to be, it is up to me."

For those of you, who are concerned that I have focused on money a little too much, please understand that money is a source of energy. Money allows you to be free and to help others:

"You can't feed the humble when you're one of them."

Over two years ago, I met my wonderful husband, Dr. Scott Peterson, and he has encouraged me to spread my story and the gift of Heartfelt Network Marketing to as many people as humanly and technologically possible. Everyone deserves to have options in life and a chance to reclaim their hopes and dreams. I want you to know what it is like to feel free, and to be able to help your elderly parents, pay for your children's college education, or contribute to a cause you are passionate about. To this end, later this year I am publishing my book entitled, *Beyond the Red Doors: The Dawn of Heartfelt Network Marketing*. I explain how I worked my way up from poor beginnings and without a college education to create the lifestyle of my dreams through Heartfelt Network Marketing. I am passionate about helping people, and I want you to know that there is more than one network marketing philosophy available to you.

I don't have a traditional college degree, but I believe that I've earned a Ph.D. in life—and now it is my turn to pay it back. ■

SHAUNA EKSTROM *was born in Mesa, AZ. and grew up in Salt Lake City, UT. She graduated Beauty College at 17 years old and also married that same year. She spent 34 years as a hairdresser and a salon owner. In the last half of her career, while in rural Washington, a 31-year marriage ended, so the need to build another income stream was essential. After 8 years of part time networking, she was able to sell her salon and go full time with her current company in the network marketing profession, and is a published author. She is the proud mother of 3 grown children and enjoys spending time with her 3 granddaughters. She and her husband, Dr. Scott F. Peterson, travel the world helping other people to realize their dreams.*

Shauna Ekstrom
www.ShaunaEkstrom.com

Taking Down Picket Fences
Kelli Estes

Failure is never a planned event. In fact, I have never met anyone who openly professes an intentional plan to fail. Growing up, you don't have thoughts about how to navigate bad choices or the repercussions that accompany those decisions. If anything, we have a mental list of what constitutes perfection, how we perceive things will turn out. I like to think of it as the "picket fence" mentality. We convince ourselves that we will be different and somehow escape life's hurts and hang-ups.

Well into my young adult years, I was making great strides toward checking off many accomplishments on my proverbial list. I graduated nursing school, purchased my first new car, found the man I would marry, delivered a healthy baby girl, built a beautiful new home, and then became addicted to pain medication. How could this be happening to me? I came from a great family that always taught me right from wrong. I am a nurse for goodness' sake! How is it possible for my happily ever after to be turned upside down like this?

Real life can be hard sometimes, and too often the perception we have becomes our reality. However, the hard knocks end up being the very blows that sober us for finding truth. On March 6, 2000, my life collided with a series of truths that began a process of change forever altering every facet of who I am today. The picket fence surrounding my little world of perfection had to be taken down.

I awakened on the morning of March 6th to realize I could no longer live life on my terms. I had recognized my secret addiction for many months but had no idea how to get help. I recall thinking I would die very young if I continued down this path, and I was terrified to even think of uttering the word "addiction" out of my mouth. I was paralyzed in fear that my career in nursing would soon be over. Co-workers held growing concern that I was impaired while caring for patients. They were right, and I knew immediate action would be required to minimize the repercussions. The pressure was intense knowing that others were onto my secret. I was living in constant fear and needed a safe place of refuge to run and hide. With the walls closing in, I prayed and asked God to help me. My prayer was nothing fancy or very deep, but more like a cry for help from a frightened little child in desperate need.

By day's end, many details fell into place allowing me to confess my hidden secret to my husband and my parents. My family was a much-needed support system and I knew the truth had to start with them. The weight of the world was lifted from my heart once I freely shared the burden I had been shouldering on my own. I self-reported my addiction to the hospital where I practiced as a registered nurse, and I filed the appropriate paperwork for a medical leave. I was also in touch with the Kentucky Board of Nursing for advice on how to navigate as an impaired nurse. This was the beginning of a very lengthy process—a three-year transformation! Three years, because that is the length of time I was accountable to the nursing board. I was entering into a covenant of sorts to protect my nursing license by following a legal agreement.

The agreed order:

- Meet with an investigator from the KBN (Kentucky Board of Nursing) quarterly.
- Complete eight weeks of outpatient drug counseling.
- Call a 1-800 line daily for random drug screening for the duration of three years.
- Attend weekly NA (Narcotics Anonymous) meetings and provide documentation.

- Work with restrictions to narcotic access.
- Pay $1000 civil penalty.

Keeping my end of the deal with the signed agreed order was an important part of my recovery. I was accountable for my own mistakes, and not following through would be my fault; there would be no room for blaming anyone else. I would not have chosen prescription drug addiction as the means to my end, but I learned lessons for my life that could not be taught any other way. I ultimately had to be stripped of my pride and become fully aware that I didn't have all the answers to life. In fact, I had very few. I had been on a journey of success where achievement was all about me. I had no thought or desire to serve others, especially if there were no obvious perks for my own self-service. I was the epitome of self-centeredness! Come to find out, self-centeredness is central to all addictions.

Shortly after signing the agreed order with KBN, the hospital where I worked posted a new position for a clinical documentation specialist. This was a brand new position that nobody knew a great deal about, but I applied for the job because it just made sense given my current circumstances. The job entailed concurrent medical record reviews and working closely with the medical staff to obtain improved clinical documentation. I got the job and, little did I know, this would serve as training for my future consulting position! All things really do work out for the good of those that love the Lord! (Romans 8:28 [NIV]) And we know that in all things God works for the good of those who love Him, who have been called according to his purpose.

Celebrating fourteen years drug free, I am ecstatic to share how thankful I am for my drug addiction! Never did I think those words would flow from my broken heart, but it's true. I deconstructed so many things about myself over those three years of restriction and in the years to follow. I have always been a hard worker with no problem setting and achieving goals, but I lacked the character required to maintain high levels of success. I engaged in a lot of personal growth during this time to become the very best person I could be. I attended small group Bible studies and stayed very connected with my church. The NA meetings unveiled the many character flaws I possessed. Eight weeks of counseling sessions taught me so much by digging down to the foundation of my life.

It was during this season that I looked in the mirror and learned to accept myself for who God created me to be. The eyes of my heart were opened to my need for Jesus and the forgiveness only He can bring. Everything about my life began changing at the very core. I was being filled with love and compassion for other people that I simply could not explain! I found myself more aware of situations in and around my sphere of influence where I could be of service to others. I was experiencing change that could not be manufactured or explained in any other way than Jesus! My flawed perception of the truth began to fade away in the distance as I began yielding my heart to this new thing happening on the inside.

In the midst of change, an undercurrent of turmoil was brewing in my marriage and with our finances. My husband owned his own business during this time and things were not going very well. He was not making wise business decisions, and he was doing his best to keep everything under the radar so he would not cause more problems at home. I had strong suspicions without any way of proving my concerns right. However, it did not take a Wall Street expert to predict the financial status of the Estes household was in rapid decline. I have always been the breadwinner in the family because of having steady reliable income. I was so disappointed after having fought my own personal battles to now be in this mess. I kept asking myself what on earth had I done to deserve this lot in life?

Everything I read about marriage improvement pointed me in the direction of showing my husband respect. I could not think of one thing deserving of respect in his life. I prayed constantly for strength to get through, provision for our family, and patience to wait and trust in the Lord. Understand, I was experiencing amazing blessings from the Lord in my personal life, but I realized that an unevenly yoked marriage would limit what God could do for us as a couple. Change would be necessary from both of us. I decided my husband was holding up further blessings from God.

I began talking with God about how it would be easier to grieve my husband's death rather than continue living like we were. Things were really bad in my marriage, but in my progress I had become very disillusioned with myself once again, even in spiritual matters. While working through this time, God impressed upon my heart that my husband would be no different than I was when it comes to being broken and stripped of pride. The years of drug addiction were necessary for me to understand what was happening. God gave me the assurance needed within my heart that He was at work in my husband's life and that, like my situation, it would take time to usher him out of a place of brokenness.

This nearly took my breath, but I realized we might have to lose the business and go through some very dark days in order for God to get his attention. I suddenly understood why I had gone through my own trials first. If I had not been humbled through drug addiction I would have filed for a divorce without giving it a second thought. Our lives would have been radically different today. During these years I spent a lot of time reading the success stories of other people to glean encouragement. I learned so much from the teachings of Mr. Zig Ziglar in particular. He is what I like to think of as America's mentor! I remember taking comfort in the fact that he was 45 years old before he made the decision to surrender his life to Jesus Christ! It's never too late for any of us. I recall clinging to the hope that life really can be different.

Upon completion of my three years of restriction with the KBN, I began praying diligently for a job that would meet my financial obligations and allow for plenty of time to serve the Lord by leading a small group of youth at my church. I love young people, and being able to sow seeds into their lives was where I desired to be. I was experiencing personal growth at such a pace it was spewing out everywhere! I could not contain the excitement stirring inside my heart! My prayer life was changing the entire landscape of how I lived, and it had to be shared with others!

I am starting my tenth year with an Atlanta based company, DCBA, Inc., as a clinical documentation specialist nursing consultant. I am still in awe of the amazing job with which God has truly blessed our family! I get to travel and meet new people four days a week! I've come to realize along the way that my travels allow me the opportunity to serve the Lord wherever I go. When I was a little girl, I always dreamed of going to work on an airplane. Living God-sized dreams never seem to get old. In the early years of this job, it provided the needed space between my husband and me as he worked through his own junk. Today, my professional work and my life in Christ have grown to become one and the same. Taking the time to listen to people and really engage them opens doors no man can open. God works, and I am faithful to show up!

In God's perfect timing, my husband finally reached that sweet broken place. Leading up to this, he had lost his father suddenly, he had lost his business, and we had to sell our beautiful home on the golf course. But at the end of this long hard road, he found Jesus! I am now married to a pastor! God has been so good to restore our marriage as well as our finances. He has given us the purpose that matters to the Kingdom of God. The years of trial and tribulation grow more distant each passing year. We are truly living in His blessings daily, and those are the things money can't buy.

In the early years of self-centeredness, I would have laughed uncontrollably if anyone tried to predict the life we are now living. I'm so thankful God's ways are not our ways because He can take the big huge mess we make and turn our lives on end only to refine us with His best! Understanding forgiveness and our need for His grace is life-changing and changes everything about how we engage life personally and professionally. We now live to rescue people from the place where we once dwelled because everyone has a story. Everyone needs to know how loved they are by the one true God who created them for a powerful purpose!

KELLI ESTES. *A few minutes with Kelli, and you'll be fast friends! She loves meeting new people and sharing a word of encouragement with those who cross her path! In preparation to communicate her story well, Kelli attended CLASS Services, author and speaker training in 2004. In 2010, she completed the Effective Communication Skills training at Ziglar Corporation in Plano, Texas. Kelli is certainly no stranger to real-life crisis. She is a registered nurse of 21 years and survived prescription drug addiction that slammed her career over 14 years ago! Kelli was dangerously close to losing her marriage. In fact, she talked seriously to God about how it might be easier to grieve her husband's death. As if that wasn't enough, the financial condition of the Estes household was in such rapid decline she could literally see their lives circling the drain! Kelli and Greg will soon celebrate 19 years of marriage. Kelli can't help but chuckle when introducing her husband as Brother Greg Estes, pastor of Liberty Baptist Church. They have one daughter, Kayla, who is 17 years old. Starting her 10th year, Kelli works for an Atlanta-based company, DCBA, Inc. where she is a clinical documentation specialist nursing consultant. Kelli and her family make their home in south-central Kentucky.*

Kelli would love to speak at your next conference or women's event to share more of her story and encourage you to become the very best version of YOU! Contact her at:

Kelli Estes
k.estes@yahoo.com
270-932-1043
www.kelli-estes.com

8

My Greatest Tragedy
Is My Greatest Blessing
Phillip Hatfield

November 9, 2008, 7:24 p.m.:"HOLD ON, STEPH! Hold on tight as you possibly can." I grabbed hold of both brakes. I squeezed my front right-hand brake hard, and I stomped my right-foot brake for the back tire as hard as I could, using both brakes and gearing down too for maximum stopping power. I grabbed the clutch with my left hand, pulled it in, clicked down on the gearshift lever with my left foot, gearing down to slow us even more. I slammed down hard on the foot brake again and squeezed the hand brake harder.

I felt the front bumper of that big Ford F-350 pickup truck as it hit us on the back tire of the motorcycle. The bike began to wiggle back and forth, side to side, in a fishtail maneuver. The truck could not stop, he was running over us. The truck driver was doing all he could but he was about to run completely over the top of us. I twisted the throttle all the way down again, wide open, and fired the Harley engine all the way up to full throttle. I had no choice!

I had opened her up all the way. She was screaming with power, as that Harley engine was WIDE open. All we could do was hope the girl in the car talking on the cell phone would take her foot off the gas. If she would just get off the stinking phone and get off the gas, we would all be OK! She was staring, looking right dead at us—but not responding. It was like she could not even see us! If she would just open her doggone eyes and pay attention—I knew she would see us and STOP!

Then she floored it. Now it was pedal to the metal. She was trying to go across three of the northbound lanes of oncoming traffic, while she was still talking on the stinking cell phone, and her traffic light was red! STOP!…STOP, Lady!…PLEASE STOP! was all I could think.

I had already committed to my plan. I had no other choice! With that big truck eating up my back tire, if I did not get the bike going faster, we would be run over and be underneath it. He was right there on my tail still, with his tires squalling, screaming, burning, and smoking from him standing on his brakes trying to STOP! You could hear it. You could smell all the burning rubber of his tires. So I busted out and opened up the throttle again as wide as it would go.

The bike lifted and rose up with the front tire just barely touching the street. The back tire of my motorcycle was biting down hard and grabbing all the road it could. We were almost in a wheelie position. The engine was bellowing, roaring, and screaming. The loud sounds coming from the full throttle Harley engine and the wide open tailpipes sounded like a screaming locomotive barreling down fast and hard, full steam ahead, with its horn blasting and blowing. It was so LOUD.

I was leaning over the top of the handlebars into the wind over the front of the bike pushing the motorcycle forward with all my might. We were at maximum power—the engine screaming, horns honking, tires squealing, burning smells of the rubber tires and exhaust fumes in the air. We were at 100 percent maximum power when…it happened!

"BAM!"

BAM, Slam! CRASH! SCReeeCH!

Then you could hear it. Hissss…Hissss…Hissss…Sssssssssssss. We were hit hard! The loud sound of impact and crashing sounds of steel, the sound of the metal from the car hitting the steel frame of my motorcycle, and the sounds of all the metal hitting metal, and my body was between all the crashing steel of the car and the hard steel motorcycle frame and that scorching hot motorcycle engine and fiery hot exhaust pipe. The tires were squealing; the smoke and smells of all the burning rubber tires were thick in the air. The sounds of the crashing and crunching continued. That hot motorcycle engine was burning through my jeans and sizzling into the skin on the inside of my left knee. Oh, the pain of my knee and my thigh being crushed between the bumper of the car and the motorcycle digging deep into the flesh of my body!

We were still moving, the car crushing on in. The burning and damage to my body was getting worse, going deeper and deeper. The hot burning engine was now all the way through my jeans and burning deeply into the flesh and skin of my leg. Oh, the smell of the burning flesh and the burning rubber from tires skidding on the road. The sounds of all the squealing and screeching of tires from everyone trying to stop their cars was awful.

Stephanie went flying in the air on impact! The young girl was still-talking on her stinking phone! She kept her foot on the gas after impact, moving forward with the motorcycle and me still in her bumper! She was not backing off at all! The car's bumper was deep into the flesh on the outside of my left leg. Oh, my thigh! It snapped in half, like a twig. My femur bone broke. The bottom half attached to my knee broke through the muscle of the thigh and was driven eight inches up and into my groin, and DEEP up into my abdomen.

OH, the pain! The left side of my body was crushed, my knee broken, and my left leg embedded into the hot motorcycle engine. My left leg was broken in 27 pieces; my ankle CRUSHED into the hot motor. My left foot went straight down to the ground and was caught between the motorcycle and the pavement below. The force literally ripped my foot off at my ankle, tearing it all the way through my boot, from the heel of my foot all the way through the Achilles tendon down to the ball of my foot.

The bike and I were now going down toward the concrete pavement. The car was pushing ahead full force even as I was going down under the bumper. All my left ribs broke on impact. The bike slid on down and tumbled as it slid down the road sideways, flipping side over side. The tumbling bike was flipping with me as I hit the road skidding, sliding, and tumbling too. The bottom of my back had now broken as I continued tumbling and sliding on the pavement.

Stephanie was thrown way off the motorcycle on impact. She hit the pavement and broke her pelvis. We both continued sliding, tumbling and rolling on the concrete. Steph's body was twisting and tumbling like a rag doll! She slid and tumbled down the road, where she finally stopped. I was still tumbling, flipping, sliding, and rolling, with the motorcycle finally skidding and slowing to a stop. The motorcycle landed behind my head. I landed approximately 250–300 feet from the initial point of impact.

Shhhhhhh…It is all quiet. It was all quiet now…Shhhhh So quiet, just for a second! Everything was now all a blur. There was almost a complete silence. It was a really eerie and awkward silence! All I could hear now was a ringing in my ears and head. I could hear the hissing of the motorcycle, the rumble of the Harley motor, the hisssssss as fuel dripped down from the gas tank and ripped fuel lines. It was hitting and splattering on the hot engine and exhaust pipes.

SPIZZZ, spizzz…It sizzled louder and faster. The smells now all mixed in with the other odors in the air of the burning rubber. The spizzz, spizzz, splattering by my head, and that deep idling Harley rumbling sound. The smell of the gas was so sharp and crisp in the air as it was pooling by my head on the pavement.

That eerie quiet…I could not hear very well, just the faint noises and voices in the background. I was dazed. My head was RINGING. Things sounded muffled, and there were loud whistles and noises in my head too, the ringing noise in my ears getting louder and louder as I could hear less and less what was going on. It is completely and totally impossible and inconceivable to explain the sounds and the atmosphere at the time. You just had to be there to experience it.

I could hear Stephanie way off in the distance behind me. She was screaming, crying and wailing, begging for someone to come and help her. She was closer to the point of impact as cars were now stopping.

She was lying on that hard, cold concrete street screaming at the top of her lungs. My heart sank to my toes as I heard her scream—and I could not help her! "Oh, My God, what have I done to Stephanie?" She was screaming and crying out as loud as she could, "Doctor, someone call the doctor, get me a doctor, PLEASE! Someone, help me, please! PLEASE HELP ME!"

The experience was surreal. I was in pain, yet I felt so guilty at that instant; I knew I was responsible for Stephanie, and I let her get hurt on my watch, on my motorcycle! Oh, my God, what have I done to her! How badly did I let her get hurt? The thought whizzed by very quickly in my head while I was coming to grips with what was going on. It was like a nightmare!

The experience was way more than possibly could ever be described. The massive, excruciating, gut-wrenching, agonizing pain was more than I thought was humanly possible to bear! My mind was rushing; my heart was jumping, pounding, and thumping, beating hard and slamming inside up against my chest. My body was quivering, jerking, and shaking uncontrollably! I knew what had just happened; yet, I did not really comprehend what had just happened at all! Everything was all such a blur!

Then, an even more excruciating, throbbing heart beat pain was now blasting hard down on my chest. I felt my heart beat all over my body from head to toe as I was shaking uncontrollably. I felt my heart beat banging, pounding, and racing all over my body. I felt my pulse as it was throbbing and beating hard in my neck too. The agonizing pain was building. I felt my heart beating harder in my chest, my back, thigh, leg, and foot. I felt my heart beat all over my body. It felt like it was busting to get out of my body.

THE PAIN!

Oh, my back hurt so badly and I could not breathe in at all; I could not take in a full breath. The pain was so acute, trying to suck in air; it was almost impossible. All my ribs were broken, I felt like I was suffocating. I was sucking in for air over and over, but there was very little air coming in. Each breath I took was just a tiny, slight sucking of air. It was so unbelievable; I was suffocating!

I tried to see what happened, and all I could see clearly was deep, dark crimson, thick red blood; it was everywhere I looked! There was blood all over the place—in the road, all over me. I saw pools and streams of blood running, channeling away from me through the lines of the concrete street. Then I realized! It was mine! I was bleeding out, right there in the street!

I was not sure anyone saw me. I didn't know if anyone was even close by. I was all alone. I was not able to get a strong enough breath to cry for help. I tried to scream out but nothing came out. I reached up and stretched out my right arm. I lifted it up to the sky high as I could, hoping someone would see me here in the distance away from the accident. I cried out as loudly as I could, "Ambulance!"

Again, in as loud a voice as possible, but since I could not breathe it wasn't very loud. It was not much louder than a whisper. I knew I had to scream if I wanted anyone to hear me, so I cried out again "AMMBUULAANNCE!…"AMMBUULAANNCE!!!!! "I raised my right arm up to the sky again, high as I could reach, looking for help, and praying too. Oh, God, help me, please. Am I going to die right here? Please, Lord, forgive me for all my sins. Take care of my son Jeremy and my mom and dad. Forgive me, please. Then I cried out again, loud as I could, "AMBULANCE!!!"

As I lay there on that ice-cold street, I knew I was going to die there all alone. I knew it was over. I was dying! I could hear the people out there but I could not check it out. I was just lying there all broken up! I felt my heartbeat beating in my head and eyeballs. My view was so distorted. I was just lying there trying to figure it all out as best I could. What happened? What is going on? Is this REAL? Nothing was making any sense to me.

Everything was just fuzzy, spinning all around, spinning faster and faster, moving up and down in all weird directions. All the colors and everything were blending together; everything was so scrambled up in my head. I could not think at all or collect my thoughts. All I remember at that moment was, "I just hurt Stephanie. How is she? Is she going to live?" My vision was way out of my control. I did not know what my surroundings were. I literally had just been knocked into oblivion! I was lying there thinking, "What just really happened to me?" What is really going on? Is this all really for real?

The relentless pain was so bad, and I was so tired. I knew my blood was still pouring out all around me as I got weaker and more tired each second. I knew I was bleeding out and that I was dying. I now was welcoming the time for the pain to end and everything to make sense. I was ready to let go. The pain was just unbearable and could no longer keep me awake! I began fading in and out, losing consciousness, not understanding anything that was happening. But it really didn't matter to me anymore! It was time to lie back and give in to it! I knew it was getting close to time for me to lay back and surrender my life. It was time to let go. Just close my eyes, and go to sleep. Then the pain would all be gone and I would be in heaven.

****

Today I live as a disabled man, an amputee! I have many health problems to overcome daily, yet I have so many blessings from my tragedy too.

We all face the "Challenges of Change." We all have struggles, obstacles, and barriers to overcome. Yes, I have overcome and still "I am overcoming daily" the changes in life. We have to work at making things better; we need a system and a plan. We also need relationships and support. The best way to "GET" is to GIVE. Go and serve someone else who has a need, and you'll find that your need will either be much less than you thought or you'll find a lot of your own solutions.

When we are active and "Doing," we begin to see results and answers. "Motion Creates Emotion," and when we start getting emotionally involved, we find solutions. We begin to see new possibilities and options instead of wallowing around in our own self-pity of being disabled or at the end of our rope.

Never get into the negativity of being in a struggle or a problem, because these pain points and painful times are when we begin to grow and create solutions. Our problems create an open door for new and creative ideas. These are the times when innovations and inventions are envisioned and dreams are born. New inventions are from people trying to solve a problem! Our tragedy or problem is sometimes the catalyst to start a whole new industry. So dream, think, surround yourself with good people, read, study—look for solutions.

I believe that "If we will do the possible, then God will do the impossible." For me, being an encourager brings me significance, pleasure, and self-worth—knowing I have gone through tough things to help other people get through their tragedies, changes, and challenges of life and business.

Through my tragedy I met my wonderful bride Erika who is the most wonderful woman in the world. I was divorced for 22 years and finally found the love of my life, and I have two wonderful kids and a family that I always dreamed of.

In my tragedy and changes of life I now have the opportunity and privilege to work for the Zig Ziglar Corporation as a speaker and business coach. I get to speak to businesses, associations, churches, schools, and prisons sharing hope and encouragement and overcoming the challenges and changes of life and business. I get the awesome privilege to encourage people and prove to them "we can all overcome our struggles, obstacles, or barriers in life or in business. Not only can we survive, we can thrive.

We need to dream again! Then create a goal and a plan for how to achieve our dreams and goals. Then when we hit that bump in the road, we have a plan and tools to help us overcome it. We need to build genuine and meaningful relationships to carry us through.

All of us have tough things that we go through in life and business—no exceptions. In my tragedy I received a gift, the gift of life. I live each and every day with more passion and purpose than ever before. I know that every breath I take is a gift, and every relationship is a blessing. I hope this story inspires you to want to know more. I would love to share more with you or your group. If I can ever help you in any way, please let me know.

My Greatest Tragedy really has been my Greatest Blessing.
—Phillip Hatfield

There is more to this story and so much more in my other two books: *Lead Like a Transformer* and *Carried By Angels*.

 **PHILLIP HATFIELD.** *Experiences in life and business have taught Phillip Hatfield that when you get knocked down, you have to GET UP! As Zig Ziglar would say, "It's time for a check-up from the neck up." Phillip has learned to overcome struggles, barriers, obstacles and roadblocks to succeed in life and business. He has learned to surround himself with great people and teams, and to get a plan, work his plan, and "Get up, get back in the game to overcome any obstacle!" Phillip says "adversity creates new opportunity and new inventions." Phillip is an amputee from a devastating accident on November 9, 2008. He was not expected to live and almost died seven times in the first ten days. He knows what it is like to have the fight of his life and "fight to live." He has learned how to overcome tragedy, obstacles and barriers in his personal life too.*

With over 30 years' experience as a leader in business and the community, from entrepreneurship to working with great companies of all sizes from all over the globe, Phillip realizes that people are business's greatest asset and resource! Known as the "turn-around guy," he has helped businesses create and execute a new plan of action to achieve success and profitability through a 180° turnaround, not only in business but in life as well. Phillip started in the restaurant and hotel business taking over the Ramada Inn Central in Fort Worth, Texas, 45 days after a fire in which five people died and 33 were severely injured. Against all odds, he and his team rebuilt the buildings and built a thriving business, "overcoming tragedy, obstacles and barriers." Phillip's success does not mean that he has not experienced adversity and failure. Phillip Hatfield's success lies in his "attitude of gratitude and appreciation," knowing he is blessed to be alive. His passion is to share the message he's learned from life, business, and Zig Ziglar's programs. And his message is crystal clear. It's all about desire, hope, encouragement, and attitude.

Phillip Hatfield
www.PhillipHatfield.com
phatfield@ziglar.com

9

WOW! How has my journey landed me here?

Alvin Johnson

Most of us wake up at some point and say to ourselves, "What happened?" or: "How did I wind up here?"

Well, that's really what I want to focus on. Simply because we all have a story, and we all have had choices to make, and all of us are where we are based on the decisions we've made to those choices—good, bad, or indifferent. I believe that our dream is right in front of us; it is never too late to begin from where we are, and we need encouragement from time to time; we need to be told that our best days are ahead of us, so don't give up. What I want to emphasize through this chapter is simple: Do not be a quitter, do not give up. It doesn't matter where we came from or where we start; it's all about the journey and how you can find your purpose while impacting other people's lives in a positive way because of the journey.

I've heard it said, "Dream Big or Go Home," and if you're going to dream big, then go after it. It doesn't matter what steps you take. Start with little steps and just keep going; chip away at that dream and be persistent. I personally struggle with seeing the big picture. I really believe that I'm gifted with the ability to see things that are not as they can or should be. The downside to this is that, because I see the big picture and I'm always going after it, sometimes I don't see the pitfalls that exist between here and there.

This is where a good example (a model or mentor) would help us navigate those pitfalls and give us an opportunity to learn from someone else's mistakes or successes.

I have been asked; "What motivates me and gets me up in the morning?" I think that the thought of, and possibility of success is my motivator. Success is perceived in many different forms; however, my greatest success would come from being a good father or a good example to my son. I've always thought that I've been a good father, and my son will say that as well, but I know I haven't always been a good example. When we think about the next generation in our business or the next generation of our family, we want them (our kids) to do better than we did. So, in my endeavor to be a better example, while never quitting and always being persistent, having faith and believing that God has a plan for all our lives, a plan for us to prosper and to have hope of a future I continually think about how I should put things in place so that my kid and his kids can have a platform from which to start that's better than where I started.

My parents were amazing at doing what they knew how to do—and that was to educate. In spite of being educators, I believed years ago that they did not have all the tools necessary to position our family to go forward from where they left off; or, if they did, I wasn't listening. In spite of those things, we as individuals have to make a choice that it doesn't matter where we start from; what matters is what we choose to do with our lives and how we do it.

That desire to succeed embraces every area of my life, and it's important because I believe it comes from a dream that's so lofty—more than I could ever accomplish on my own—that it's God-inspired. I believe the reason it wakes me, and that I'm so passionate about this, is that it's not about me. Rather, it's about the things I've been through, the things that I'm going through, and how they are designed by God to help other people. As I mentioned earlier about being a good example, it feels as though I'm treading a road that few people have traveled, and therefore I'm making the journey easier for those who come behind me. Hopefully, I'm going in the right direction. (Humor)

The passion and desire to help comes from my background in real estate. Being a mortgage broker\banker for 15-plus years, I have witnessed clients and the general population acquiring mortgages that they didn't truly understand. The lack of consumer knowledge in this area fueled my desire to educate my clients through their process. And then this evolved into the realization that everyone may not have the opportunity to become a homeowner, so maybe there is a platform with which we can utilize our gained experience to perpetuate that dream.

Now, here at Hope Housing Foundation (HOPE), we believe that until a family has reached the point in their lives when they wish to become a homeowner, or even if they never do, they are "entitled" to live in a safe, decent, sanitary, affordable environment. So today, I am president (What?!) of Hope Housing Foundation, a 501(c)3 nonprofit affordable housing provider that provides housing for the economically disadvantaged singles, families, seniors, and students in the communities we serve. Along with providing housing, we put together programs to enhance the lives of our residents. So, to backtrack a little bit and answer the "What wakes me up" question again, it's a desire to succeed. And that success comes through empowering other people to make better decisions, or empowering other people to live to their fullest potential, because of experiences I've had or knowledge I've gained.

I'm often asked about my training or where I went to school. I'm not a college graduate. Actually, I've never gone to college, but I did work at a college. My parents were teachers, and one of my grandmothers was an elementary school principal. So I've been around smart people my whole life, and I opted, because of fear, to not attend school. I'm not sure what I was afraid of, but, I as I think back, it may have been the fear of rejection or a fear of failing. Because of that decision, I have felt throughout the years that I didn't have anything I could fall back on. It's often said: "Well, I've got my education to fall back on. I can always go do what

I want to do, and if that doesn't work out I can come back to my degree field and always get a job." The only thing I've had to fall back on was my work ethic and a principle that my dad taught me: A good man will always have a job. It may be cutting grass, it may be picking up trash, but a good man will always be a provider for himself and for his family.

I began my career in real estate as a painter's helper; then I got promoted to painter. I can tell you that it didn't feel like a career at that time. After knocking on quite a few doors because I needed to make more money, I then began calling myself a "Big Time" paint contractor. It seemed that most of my prospective clients needed work done on their home before painting, and I had a few friends in all the building industry trades. I immediately went from paint contractor to general contractor. After a few years of this, and a move to the big city of Houston in the early 1990s, I began to buy distressed houses. My philosophy was "One man's trash is another man's treasure." I've done that for the last 25 years and continue to do so as a hobby today. Our apartments are purchased using the same philosophy. I personally do it as a hobby.

After several years of contracting and cultivating a relationship with an acquaintance, who ultimately became a close friend. I had an opportunity to help him with his dream of becoming a business owner and opening a mortgage company. Today that sounds so admirable, but that wasn't the purpose back then. The reason this was so attractive was that I had borrowed a lot of money buying and fixing houses, so this could be an opportunity to go "Big." Along with the mortgage company, I gained an unimaginable amount of knowledge that I use every day—and that propelled me from what I was then to what I am now.

Early in life as a teenager, I developed a relationship with Christ, but for many years I lived as though that relationship didn't exist. Grace and mercy have followed me, and I'm living testimony of God's goodness. and I'm living testimony of God's goodness. One day I realized that if I wanted to advance in my career, have a better family life, and be a better person, I needed a mentor. For the first time in my life I felt as though it was me against the world, maybe because things weren't going so well and I was tired. In the process of praying for God to bless this hand-picked mentor ("unknown at this time"), I was again reminded that God has a plan for all of us.

I began to pray for mentors in several areas of my life—and they came. One is a family man who had been married 40-plus years; I needed him because I hadn't succeeded in that area. I needed a business mentor because I had had several businesses that hadn't been as successful as planned; I just didn't know how to take them to the next level. So I do believe that God spoke to me and gave me this dream because I actually prayed that my passion would become my purpose—or, better yet, that my purpose would become my passion. And I truly believe that, as I evolved into this different or better-informed person as a result of my growth as a Christian, through my real estate experiences and mortgage background, I discovered a portion of my purpose.

Not having a fallback plan has motivated me or pushed me to continue "walking by faith and not by sight." Having gained this mortgage information and gone through these hard-knock experiences and "figuring it out" on my own in turn gives the next person an opportunity to learn from my successes and failures, and thus have a better outcome.

Well, my prayer for a mentor led me in a direction I could have never imagined. As I grew in the mortgage business, I hit a brick wall in 2007; plus, my second marriage was failing. I closed my mortgage company to move to another city to follow my wife, who was chasing her dream—little did I know, her dream was to get away from me. I had lived in this city before, so I began to reach out to some old contacts. One of my friends, not knowing what I had prayed for, introduced me to my next mentor. (I know this sounds "spiritual," but I had literally just spoken to God about this, as He is my friend who sits next to me all the time).

This "mentor to be" just happened to be the founder and president of a large nonprofit housing foundation that owned approximately 16,000 apartments. After this initial meeting, he said: "Alvin, call me, and I'll help you do anything you want to do." So I did call him, and he answered—the first time. I ran a deal by him and he didn't like it; he said:

"Nope, Alvin, that's not going to work." Inevitably, I had to pursue this relationship, so I called this guy for a year and a half. Once a week, twice a week, I called, sent him emails, texted—you name it. Finally, after a year and a half, he answered my call again and said: "Alvin, I am so tired of you calling me and emailing me. I've never seen anyone as persistent as you. You said you wanted to learn, and you've hounded me for a long time." The phone went silent for moment, and then he said: "If you really want to know what we do, come to Amarillo for 30 days. I'll put you up. If you like it, then we'll figure out how I can help you."

Back to the persistence thing. For a year and a half, I prayed for mentors, and this guy came into my life. He was exactly what I thought I wanted as a business mentor at that time. And he said he would help me; but then I had to pursue him. And the pursuit led to Amarillo, Texas, for 30 days. After 30 days he sat me down in his office and said: "Alvin, you've been here 30 days; what are you going to do now?" I said: "Well, I'm not leaving until you send me home." For the next twelve months I spent a lot of one-on-one time with this man in board meetings, investor meetings, and touring all the properties. He gave me carte blanche access to everything in the foundation.

Thirteen months after I arrived in Amarillo, he died in a car accident. Because I had spent so much time with him and had really become a student of everything to which he had allowed me access, the board of directors of a billion-dollar housing foundation asked me to take his seat. So I went from a non–college graduate, a two-time failed marriage guy, to the president of a billion-dollar foundation—overnight.

Well, to some it would appear to be overnight, but this progression of walking, learning, training, pushing through tough times, took 30-plus years. It was one step leading to another step, to another step—and I ended up in that seat. I accepted the position knowing that the organization was in bankruptcy. We knew that there were challenges ahead. The organization had over 400 employees, 40 of them in the corporate office. Shortly thereafter, through attrition and the bankruptcy, we got the corporate office down to a core of about eight employees.

With the guidance of an attorney, we sat around a table every day and wrote a Chapter 11 reorganization bankruptcy plan for this billion-dollar foundation. We worked with some of the most notable bankruptcy attorneys in the country to unwind the web of entities involved in the ownership of 66 apartment complexes, each of which had three or four entities involved in the ownership of that one complex. There were approximately 250 companies owning 66 complexes, employing 400-plus employees. After that plan was adopted by the court, I was fired.

This was another opportunity to feel sorry for myself, but I knew that wouldn't help. After I was fired, I prayed and asked God for direction for my life and what I should do next. A dear friend who I met through that experience and who was the president of another organization told me: "Alvin, here's another nonprofit. It has 15 years' experience in affordable housing. There are no assets here, but you can take this organization and mold it into what you want to do with it."

So, another close friend and I would sit down every day and say: "I hope this, I hope that. I hope we can do this, I hope we can do that. We hope this happens." Finally we decided to name this new organization "Hope Housing Foundation." We knew it was going to take a miracle and prayer and all the hope we could muster for this thing to be successful. We had in excess of seven million dollars' worth of pending lawsuits, and our 501(c)3 status had been revoked by the IRS. We were informed that this status is never reinstated, but we were determined to hope, determined to pray, and determined to fast and believe God, that He could make it happen.

Two and half years later we settled that seven-million-dollar lawsuit for five thousand dollars with no fault. We got our 501(c)3 exemption back, and the IRS accepted our returns as filed. Through persistence, prayer, hope, and all those things we set our mind to do, it came together. Either the wheels were going to fall off or we were going to win. Here we are today, six years after my first day in Amarillo. That was March 30th, 2008. On April 1st, 2009, my mentor died in that car accident, and here I am five years later in McKinney, Texas, and Hope Housing Foundation owns close to 1,000 apartments. We've put together our own team of employees, individuals who have the ability to hope and believe in something bigger than themselves, bigger than all of us together.

The close friend who sat with me is now the financial manager of Hope Housing Foundation. She was a young mother at age 16; she went on to finish high school; and she began to pull herself up and work her way through junior college. I met her when she was a volunteer resident board member of the other housing foundation. Because she volunteered as a "Wise Woman" for a charitable function on the property, she did not have to pay rent. She volunteered her time and talents, which were her treasures, to make other people's lives better, in spite of what she was going through herself. From the uncomfortable position of being a young single mom with three kids, with nothing but hope that her future would be anything other than living an economically challenged lifestyle, her choice to volunteer and give back has made her life all the better. Today she's 34 years old and the financial manager of our multi-million-dollar foundation.

That's the kind of impact we want to make across the board, across the globe, in every community that we own. Today, as we carry on our own mission at Hope Housing Foundation, I encounter families who desire to buy a home one day, but there is also a population of individuals who cannot fathom the notion of homeownership. There are many instances where we have four generations of family members living at or below the poverty level. There is a 63-year-old great-grandmother, a 46-year-old grandmother, a 30-year-old mother, a 16-year-old child who's pregnant and about to bring a fifth generation into a cycle that will never change. We endeavor to educate the tenants of the community that there is something different out there for them. We try to inform the population that they don't have to live like this, that there are other options.

I'm a guy who didn't go to college; I'm a guy who has had some really hard life experiences because of choices that I made—and now I'm an ambassador of hope. It proves that your life can change, but it all starts with you. So that's the fuel behind the dream and the passion.

We probably all have a dream, but we each have to choose to follow that dream. We have to make a choice to get up in the morning. We must choose persistence—quitting is not an option. We must believe in ourselves. But there is one last point that I believe is critical to all our successes. It's the power of our relationships with other people, "alignment." My pastor, Reverend Keith Craft of Elevate Life Church, likes to call it our "Family of Choice." You must surround yourself with other people who are like-minded or people who think the way you think (to some degree), who believe the way you believe.

The Bible provides us with several examples where the alignment of some strong believers, people who had enough faith to believe for someone else, caused that person to be healed or delivered. Even though you have a dream, and you had the faith to get started, you must align yourself with friends who can and will carry you through a period in time when you have become tired and may not be able to believe that what you have begun will ever come to fruition. We all experience days like that. We all have a story, but if you can relate to where I came from, and see where I am today, hopefully, it will bring some form of encouragement for your journey. And that's what it's all about. ▪

ALVIN JOHNSON *is the president of Hope Housing Foundation (HOPE) and Assertive Management Group, LLC. The foundation, which is headquartered in McKinney, Texas, was incorporated as a 501(c)3 in 1998. HOPE has a business model that positions it as one of the most effective nonprofit affordable workforce housing organizations in the country.*

Before fully investing his time into HOPE, Alvin was the vice president of operations for the American Housing Foundation in Amarillo, Texas, (AHF); he also served as interim president for two years. The Amarillo-based American Housing Foundation successfully grew from two apartment complexes purchased from a local Catholic organization in 1989 to one of the largest affordable housing companies in the country, providing homes to more than 50,000 families and individuals, while supporting healthy communities. The American Housing Foundation boasts 16,000 units spread across Texas (including nine apartment complexes in the Austin area) and other states. Alvin's tenure with AHF helped grow the vision of what Hope Housing Foundation is and will become.

Alvin's focus has not always been on multifamily units. His start in the housing market began in December of 1999 in the single-family home sector. He served as president as well as chief executive officer for the Houston, Texas, based companies, Wholesale Lending Exchange, Inc., and Near Town and Associates, as well as the De Soto, Texas, based ADJ Mortgage, LLC. These companies provide mortgage services for commercial and residential properties, investment firms, business entities, and nonprofit organizations within the State of Texas. The companies originate, process, close, and service mortgage loans.

Mr. Johnson takes pride in being an industry leader in service and building strong relationships with his business partners. Through his faith and determination, Hope Housing Foundation will definitely be a front runner in the affordable housing market.

Alvin Johnson
Hope Housing Foundation

7290 Virginia Parkway
Suite 2300
McKinney, Texas 75071
806-372-(HOPE)4673
214-842-8075

10

The Traveling Three
Wiley Kisling

Three tips to guide you through your travels in life—
and to share with others whenever you feel so inspired!

My growth as an individual has required that I pave an environment of positivity. Discovering new avenues of happiness drives my success forward. A constant urge for peace produces a smooth path wherever I trek. But how did I get here? The road to prosperity has been a long one, and I'm still winding my way around curves, through tunnels, and over rickety bridges. It has been a thirty-year expedition and I'm just getting started.

As a young boy, I began to notice I was different. Not in a subtle "that one is shy" sort of way. No, I was strikingly different in a physically loud and visually obvious way. It never struck me as a negative though. I always found it fascinating that people were so interested in me, even though I felt no different from any other person. I was incredibly fortunate to be raised in a home full of love, respect, and kindness. I have always felt level with my peers and able to explore just as much territory, despite having limited mobility.

My sturdy home life allowed me to appreciate the outside world while exploring unfamiliar locations. I am a fearless traveler as long as I have a companion. I've been fortunate enough to travel many places both inside and outside the United States. Travel in general is a bit easier these days, but it's no less wondrous. Whether it's the luxury of a cruise ship suite or a flooded tent in sub-zero temperatures, I've experienced it—and I have loved every moment. It can be a little unnerving for me, being carried by strangers up flights of stairs or over an ocean floor, but there is something great about sharing in triumph.

The first adventure I can recall is with a friend from across the street. We packed up a wagon together with toys, snacks, and extra hats in case the weather turned ugly. I sat in the wagon and my friend pulled me all the way around the block. It may not seem like far, but to us it was the Wild West and we were conquering new land. Being a paraplegic did not seem limiting because the company I kept believed in me and viewed me as an equal. We gave each other the confidence to keep going all the way around the block, something neither of us would have dared to do alone. Through friendship, we achieved greater heights than we would have on our own. I still think about this moment in my life and how it has shaped my outlook.

No matter one's outlook, things don't always go as planned in life, especially when traveling. This leads me to my second story of adventure. I've had less than perfect experiences, even among phenomenal company. Airports do a wonderful job catering to people with special needs, but mistakes do happen. The vast majority of my journeys have gone without a hitch, but one experience will always stick out in my mind. When I board an airplane, my wheelchair is stowed with the luggage after I am seated. Then upon arrival it is brought up to meet me. This has happened without failure—except once. You can imagine my surprise and frustration when my body took one flight and my wheelchair took another! That's exactly what happened when I went to visit my relatives on vacation one year.

I was thousands of miles from home and without my second half. I was naked. I can tell you that one thing people don't understand about wheelchair-bound folks is that the chair becomes an extension of our body. In this moment of complete helplessness, I almost panicked, and I may well have had a breakdown were it not for the support of my family. It is humbling to have your independence taken away. We were all very tense for a day or so until my chair finally arrived at its proper destination. It's amazing how creative you can get under pressure. I had to get carried here and there, borrow a wheelchair from the airport, and use a spare office chair with rollers just to get around. I could have let this event ruin my vacation, but I think I picked up some valuable lessons from it.

When things do go right, it's possible to soar to new heights. My final excursion I want to share with you took me to a place more beautiful than I could have ever imagined—across the ocean and into Alaska. I experienced something I will never forget. After many days of travel by sea, my family and I reached the friendly northern state, but the pilgrimage didn't end at the ship's quay. It would be easy to stop and simply enjoy the local tourist destinations, but we were all looking for something special this trip. We wanted to get a different perspective, and in order to do that we would have to get ourselves some wings.

There are so many ways to travel, but there is nothing quite like flying. After exploring our options between seaplanes and helicopters, my father and I decided to see the glaciers with a small group in a helicopter. It's no small task getting in and out of a helicopter without the use of your legs but, as always, I found myself surrounded by people more than willing to help make it happen. It was a cloudy day and as we flew through the mountain ravines it began to softly snow. White clouds covered the mountains and our path seemed uncertain, but it was magnificent all the same. I began to wonder if this was the safest decision. After several minutes of flying blindly, the clouds cleared and we saw nothing but beautiful blue blocks of ice and lush green mountains. It was crisp and clear from then on. Looking down from the window, I could see where the ice met the earth and the dark crevasses in the ice that seemed to go down forever. Our pilot told us we would be landing right on one of the glaciers down below us. It was thrilling, but also a bit unnerving.

As we approached the glacier I thought how incredible it was that I could make it this far out into the serene wilderness. I was perfectly comfortable sitting in the helicopter, knowing I had landed on a glacier. That was an achievement in itself, but my father encouraged me to get out and explore. I thought it would be a futile effort—my wheels on a solid sheet of ice? I wouldn't be able to go anywhere! But he insisted by pointing out to me "how often do you get to be on a glacier?" So I jumped in my wheelchair and slid around just as awkwardly as everyone else. I got a much better view by stepping out of my comfortable helicopter seat. I took in a full 360-degree view, and I will never forget the moment I turned and saw the helicopter. I paused and thought about how many people it took to get me out of that helicopter, and from my home town in Colorado all the way to this nearly untouched oasis. The kindness and determination of others gives me strength every day, and there is no greater example of this than when I looked back at that helicopter from my wheelchair.

Along my years of wayfaring I have learned that people are very kind and sympathetic in all sorts of circumstances. We all enjoy it when we can be of help to one another. We want to share peace and positivity. Everyone around me has supported me to get me where I needed to go. I have been able to continue navigating even though sometimes I am completely without an independent means of movement. I have been able to maintain a high level of positivity through these experiences because of the help I have received from so many wonderful souls around me.

There are many elements to fostering peace and positivity. By nurturing these tenets I have been able to progress through tough times and cultivate happiness within myself. I would like to share three tips I have picked up through my travels. These are just a handful of techniques that I use regularly which seem to have high impact and relatively low effort. Share these with your fellow voyagers.

The number one tip that has helped me navigate through life: Take a vacation with your soul. Quieting the mind on a daily basis rejuvenates my soul and gives me the freedom to process information in a way that the noise of daily life tends to drown out. I like to spend ten to fifteen minutes in silence each day. This amount may drive some people crazy, so if you aren't used to it try starting out with five minutes. If you still find it to be agonizing, cut it back to three minutes for the first few days. Be consistent, but if you miss a day don't fret. This is a long-term project.

Once you have incorporated silence into your daily routine, you will be able to bring yourself to a place of calm clarity in multiple environments. I like to carry my calm wherever I go, like a set of keys to a car waiting out front that drives me to a resort any time I want. When things get tense in my day, and I feel a heavy weight building up, I'll take a moment for myself, a mini vacation. I step away from the current environment, give myself silence, and empathize with my stressors.

Empathy will lead you to happiness in unexpected ways. If you are huffing and puffing over that blockhead who cut you off on your way to work this morning, take a moment and think about that person and what might have led him to do such a thing to endanger himself. Discovering the root cause in any scenario will almost always result in a greater understanding of the situation and a larger pool of empathy to draw upon in the future. Practice your quieting, and find empathy in that moment. A quiet getaway is always just minutes away.

This leads me to my second tip. Be a tour guide. Help others throughout your day. Nothing feels better than giving another individual the ability to "fly." It's easy to get caught up in our own goals, deadlines, and other aspirations. Helping is energizing, and if you are building up your empathy muscle you'll find you have more energy and insight to achieve your own goals. Taking just a moment out of your day to help another individual will have countless benefits. If you are stuck on a problem, your motivation is starting to wane, or perhaps you are feeling immense pressure to meet a deadline, helping another individual may give you some perspective and the inspiration you need. Plus, helping others simply feels good. It will put you in a mood that is more conducive to creatively problem-solve your own circumstance. Be a guide and show the way for others. Light their path, give them a map, or hold their hand as they dive into uncharted territory.

My third and final tip is a doozy. This will require actual physical work. Are you ready for it? Go on a journey. Here is the deal: Your environment may be holding you back. Take a walk or drive, and get away from your routine. Break your cycle, whatever it may be. Monotony is the killer of creativity. Observe what's happening outside your bubble. There is a lot going on out there, believe me. If nature inspires you, take a trip to the park; but if the buzz of city life is electrifying, then head to the center of town. When we are bogged down with responsibilities, deadlines, and personal quarrels, we forget how amazing life can be. Find those places outside your normal routine that are inspiring to you, and soak them in. Go alone or take a friend. Either way, make sure you are breaking out of your normal habits. Your journey is what you make of it. If a lunch-break journey doesn't do the trick, take a weekend to reconnect with what inspires you.

I like to keep things simple in my life, and these three things are about as simple as it gets: Take a vacation, be a tour guide, and go on a journey! I've learned to use these techniques in all sorts of circumstances and they have helped me continue down a smooth road in life. Sure there are bumps, bridges, and sharp turns, but I always take a GPS and a friend. With the right tools and attitude, the road to happiness is just around the corner. ■

 WILEY KISLING *is an accomplished webmaster and social media guru who loves immersing himself in the latest technology trends and online experiences. His main form of transportation is by wheelchair due to a birth defect known as Spina Bifida. When he isn't perusing the cyber world he is passionately planning his next adventure to destinations unknown. Through his travels he has met many interesting folks, and he strives to find common ground with anyone he meets. He enjoys helping businesses and entrepreneurs build their online presence through websites, apps, and web marketing. During his free time you will find him reading about human factors and psychology as well as sharing cinematic experiences with friends.*

Wiley Kisling
wileykisling@gmail.com

Gifts, Small Victories, and Chicken Fingers

Matt Patterson

I f you ask a large group of people to give their definition of a gift, it's quite possible you would receive an even larger group of answers. Replies could range from items related to holidays, milestones, our talents, families, as well as important or life-changing events. Personally, I can say the greatest gifts I have received in this life have come from some of my greatest trials and tragedies.

Among the "gifts" I have been given in my short life I count love, tragedy, grief and redemption.

It has been 26 years since our first daughter, Emily, was born. The birth of a young couple's first child almost certainly falls under the "gift" category. After celebratory phone calls, bubble gum cigars, hugs, kisses, and laughter, we learned that Emily was born with Down syndrome. There was shock, combined with absolute dismay. The thing is, these emotions quickly gave way to joy and happiness. Our little angel was truly a gift from God.

Life was good.

However, just two years later this joy and happiness turned to heartache. A routine late-night visit to the emergency room to remedy a temperature would later reveal that our little one had leukemia. Cancer.

Down syndrome first. Now cancer!

Three-plus months of chemotherapy were followed by tests, transfusions, remission, relapse, surgery, and eventually, death. Each of these moments during Emily's treatment and life brought countless gifts. Included in these are obedience, patience, faith, strength, persistence, endurance, fellowship, and character. Incidents in our lives—big or small—develop our character. I once read a scripture that taught me such a valuable lesson: *We know that these troubles produce patience. And patience produces character.*

Our lives, as short as they may be, are a test. And one of the biggest tests we can endure is how we respond to those moments when we don't feel the presence of God in our lives. I believe deeply that one of God's greatest gifts is to teach us that there is a purpose behind every single one of our trials or problems. Treat them as a gift, an opportunity to draw closer to those who are most important to us. These problems oftentimes compel us to look toward God and to count on Him, rather than ourselves.

In his book, *The Purpose Driven Life*, Rick Warren shares: "You'll never know that God is all you need until God is all you've got." Psalm 139:12, says that Jesus offers himself as the light in our darkness. It's my prayer that you learn to have faith and trust that God can lift you in your times of peril and save those moments as gifts.

Although it was more than 20 years ago, I can still remember sitting in Emily's hospital room with knots in my stomach waiting for test results. Whether it was just for simple blood count results or for the confirmation of a clean spinal tap, there were times when the waiting was absolutely excruciating. Throughout Emily's treatment for leukemia, we would anxiously reach out and take any type of small victory we could lay our hands on.

Normal blood counts? Sign me up!

No adverse reaction to chemotherapy? Oh yeah, we'd definitely take that!

We'd give just about anything if she could have a good night's sleep.

In the day-to-day battle against this hideous disease, these small victories meant the world to us. There had to be a positive focus. I took any tiny positive and celebrated in a big way. Well, at least to us it was big. Try Burger King chicken fingers and fries—complete with the cardboard crowns.

Each and every one of us should focus on the positive and build on the momentum toward something greater. As we learn to celebrate our small victories, it creates a positive energy. As a mother, father, and also as a leader, you need to find those tiny nuggets of victory to celebrate within your family, yourself, and your organization. Find something to be happy about.

Find that one thing—that single, solitary thing to celebrate.

Discover a small victory that will lift others to push toward the next level. Reach out to them. Be there for them. Be their Difference Maker. Your adversity can be the difference in their life.

A wise mentor once shared with me that one person's problem is another person's prayer. Oftentimes, adversity can teach us so many lessons and instill habits which will assist in overcoming any challenge—individually or organizationally. Celebrate every step of the marathon because it will place you that much closer to your goal.

What is YOUR chicken fingers and fries? What is your next small victory? How will you celebrate YOUR next small victory? Last, but not least, how many cardboard crowns will you need?

In Emily's life, treatment, and in her passing, she brought me countless gifts for which I'll be eternally grateful. It has truly brought light to my darkness. Her loving nature and courage touched the hearts of everyone she met. Today, and every day, she continues to teach me and so many others to value their own life.

And that is what I call—a gift.

 MATT PATTERSON *is a highly sought-after inspirational speaker, as well as an award-winning and international best-selling author. His first published work,* My Emily, *has been an Amazon top-rated international bestseller. This debut book has also received recognition as a national award winner and finalist in the Readers Favorite Book Reviews & Awards Contest, the Next Generation Indie Book Awards, as well as the National Indie Excellence Book Awards.*

Matt's background includes 20-plus years in marketing communications, public and media relations, as well as print and broadcast journalism. In addition, he is an Air Force veteran, having earned the Air Force Commendation Medal and Air Force Achievement Award. In addition to speaking and writing, he volunteers his time helping organizations and charities dedicated to assisting families with special-needs children or children battling pediatric cancers.

To learn more about Matt and how you can bring him to speak at your next conference or event, please visit the following.

Matt Patterson
www.my-emily.com
www.mattpatterson.me.
matt@mattpatterson.me.

It's the Journey!
Heidi Poche

This is the story of a girl with chestnut hair, a little nose sprinkled with freckles, and blue eyes who loved to draw. Drawing was my escape. From the time I can remember, I identified with being an artist. I relished the accolades when I drew a likeness to nature or a person. In fact, one of my first entrepreneurial adventures at seven or eight years old was selling my caricature drawings to neighbors. As I recall, I only sold one—but it was enough to spark a fire in me. I was good at drawing and painting—not exceptional, but good. I was always eager to learn more. That's where I believe "great" is possible: always being curious and asking questions. While still in college, I had the privilege of using a bit of my artistic talent and a lot of hard work to apprentice under a local decorative artist. Although it was important that I earn a living, my primary concern was getting it right.

I started my own business in my junior year of college. It seemed the natural progression as I look back. It was very organic and not necessarily a system of processes I can map out for someone. A series of events just created the space for me to say, "I can do this." Pursuing my career as a decorative artist for the next 10 years was the best education for me. I won't lament my lack of guidance or forethought today. It would only serve to tarnish the memories I have of a career path that fed my soul and instilled in me an even greater desire to learn more and do better.

What happened in the past is just that. Leave it there. Only bring the lesson along for the ride. Your past doesn't define your future success.

Fast forward to my early 30s. In a very short span of four years, I had three daughters. Each child brought fulfillment and challenges. By the time I had my third daughter, I knew I wouldn't be happy with business as usual. My clients could no longer be the only ones getting my best. I now had three little human beings who deserved my attention. I was torn between a job that had been such an integral part of who I thought I was and a new job with even greater demands, a job in which I felt much less qualified—motherhood. The feeling of being overwhelmed and distractions were my daily challenges. Between the latter part of my last pregnancy and closing up shop for good, our family had experienced Hurricane Katrina, evacuation, relocation, child birth, continuing to run my husband's business, and restructuring mine.

What became increasingly clear was that I could survive. In the chaos, clarity would make brief appearances—just long enough for me to make note of what was most important to me. Sometimes there were whispers that change was necessary. Sometimes it was a jolt that halted everything until I made a decision. It took time. I had to name it before I could find a path.

Listen for the winds of change. At first, it may feel like your being tossed about, but it's necessary to propel you to the next level.

I say the Universe speaks to us, always, first in whispers.
And a whisper in your life usually feels like…
    "Hmm, that's odd."
    Or, "hmm, that doesn't make any sense."
    Or, "hmm, is that right?"
It's that subtle. And if you don't pay attention to the whisper,
    it gets louder and louder and louder.

I say it's like getting thumped upside the head.
If you don't pay attention to that, it's like getting a brick
upside your head.
You don't pay attention to that, the brick wall falls down.

—Oprah Winfrey

I was tired of being tired. I'd been pregnant for most of the previous four years. I was tired of wearing maternity clothes. I wasn't even sure I felt human most of the time. I missed the fulfillment I got from my job. This made the guilt even worse. Why would I feel more fulfillment from a job than from taking care of my own children? It wasn't the same. I needed outside stimulation. Work has always felt good to me. It's a perfect combination of frustration, accomplishment, joy, and exhaustion all in one—kind of like motherhood.

At the time, I couldn't see the good work I was doing with my children. I certainly didn't give myself enough credit. It didn't happen overnight, but, over the next 18 months after Katrina, I knew that I wanted more time with my children. I wanted to feel better physically. And having a career was essential to my well-being, both emotionally and financially. My husband was always the primary breadwinner in our household, but a growing family was putting a stress on him that I hadn't noticed in the past. During the process, I was a stay-at-home mom for about nine months. Even though the hours I shared with my children were increased, I didn't feel the quality was much better than being away at my job. In the meantime, I was on a mission to take better care of myself.

The biggest shift for me came when I tried a nutritional cleansing system. Change was imminent. I dropped the last of my baby weight and started working with a trainer. My mental clarity was renewed. I had more energy and, most of all, I saw possibility. I was searching for a new opportunity, but couldn't name it—yet. Of course, my friends began to take notice of my physical transformation. It was easy enough to share with them what I was doing. After all, I wanted everyone I knew to feel as good as I did by sharing it forward. I was introduced to the concept of network marketing, but couldn't fathom that I would be a part of it as a profession. Having said that, I still believed that finding a profession that allowed me to thrive as an individual and a mother was a good fit for me. I had to pare this new concept down to its most essential element— sharing a good idea, and maybe one that that could be life-changing.

If I told you how much I love my car! I love the remote start, the easy access, the entertainment system, the size, the ride, the leather seats, and the price. This car really makes traveling a joy. Would you be interested in taking a closer look if you were in the market for a new SUV? If you really liked my car, and I could show you how to get it for a discount, would you be interested? If you bought the car, and loved it as much as I do, would you tell a friend? In a nutshell, this is what I do. And each time I do it, my company pays me. (As of today, GMC has never sent me a check or a thank-you note.)

Thanks to the culture of my new-found company, I surround myself with people who are choosing to work together and who are always progressing. We celebrate each other's successes and examine where we can do better. The bonus is that I am creating an income that far surpasses my previous career and makes a significant impact on how we plan our family's future. I am building a business in the pockets of my day. I am so grateful that I didn't give up. This is a profession that works—if you don't give up. It's that simple. It's just that it's not the status quo. I argue that it should be.

I was an artist, mother, and wife. I was still attached to who I thought I was. I went to work to complicate a very simple concept of showing people how to feel better in their own skin, how to feel more alive, and how to see the possibilities in their own lives. I continued to ask questions, learn, grow, and stretch. One of the great things about learning this new profession is that it brought up some of the same sense of wonder and curiosity that I thrived on in my decorative painting. This time, however, I was teaching the client how to do something; that is, I was helping people identify what can make a difference in their life, and showing them a way to create that.

While contemplating how this new job would fit into my life, I kept in mind how important it was for me to make time for family, friends, and community. That had been getting more difficult to keep in balance with my previous career. Personal growth has been key. Whether or not they join my business, it's important to stay in the company of those who want more for themselves and others. You are a culmination of the five people with whom you associate the most. That is a powerful motivator. While I don't see that I have found the elusive balance, I always find possibility when I reach out. Stagnation is one of my greatest fears. Reaching out can mean calling a friend, reading a book, attending a seminar or conference. I'm more cautious of my choices as I realize they are precious commodities. They determine my state of mind, my community, and my growth to some extent. I want to be around people who are innovative and committed to providing a service or goods that will positively impact our world. At a time when I felt like I was at the end of my rope, I chose to take a leap and try something new. I used a nutritional system that boosted my body's performance and improved my mental clarity and focus.

> *Amidst the chaos, take care of yourself first. Just like on an airplane when you are supposed to give yourself oxygen first, if you don't take care of you, then there is nothing left within you to give the ones you love.*

The concept seemed simple enough. I was feeding my body high-quality, delicious food. I wanted to share! I wanted others to experience the exhilaration of a vibrant, healthy body. I knew from my own experience that I could show others how to use a system that would provide results, using a system that creates confidence—confidence that they can be successful and duplicate their results. You don't have to be an expert, as long as you are committed to learning. I reached up and out to people who were successful in this industry. What I found was that many of the most successful people were just like me! They were at a point where it became a priority to have more time for what's important in life.

Each person had a unique story as to how they arrived at this point in their life. Yet each story had a common thread—more time, without sacrificing financial security. This was something that resonated with me. This methodology has proven successful over the past six years, with the building of a team of 14,000 and growing. Having said yes to trying a product, and eventually building a business alongside my mother, has not only impacted my family's future, but is ensuring that of my mother's. We are transforming lives everyday, ours and those we reach out to. It's a model that even my children have embraced. My daughters have parents who work and thrive in an environment that includes family. It's all they know. They see that success can be achieved with passion and purpose in helping others achieve success.

Ask questions. Lots of questions! Find anyone who will support your quest, and don't feel you have to know all the answers on your own. Reach out for support! Don't leave out those who matter most.

I like to put things together. I love IKEA. If I do steps A, B, C, I will get the outcome in the picture. I suppose in life I think, sometimes, that if I read these books, if I do what they say, my life will be THAT way. I buy book after book, listening to the same advice, yet my life doesn't look like the picture! Why not?

Life is about action, not just instruction. When you let go of the idea that your profession or particular skill set defines your human worth, then you can really grow into the opportunity that is presented to you. Opportunity is what we make it. Sometimes it is staring you in the face, jumping up and down, and screaming your name. Take out your earplugs and open your eyes. It's just an offer—yes or no—but don't think that it won't change your life, either way. The regret of having passed on an opportunity to learn, grow, work, etc., can be much greater than trying and failing.

I'll use the analogy of a woman who is about to topple over from slinging yet one more bag over her shoulder. No matter how fashionable or useful it may have been in the beginning, it's added weight. How does adding on someone else's fear and judgment help you on your journey? We each came into this world with nothing but possibility. Through real or perceived events, we began to add layers. Some serve us; others weigh us down. Stepping outside your comfort zone is the best way to grow. I'm challenged every day by my children, my husband, and my job. And that's all before I add my own doubts, fears, and dreams.

> *The people you love the most may give you the most push back. Not everyone wants you to change. Some are even fearful of what "change" will mean. Forgive their fear, and press on.*

I am grateful every day that my mother didn't give in to my push-back and negativity around getting my health back on track and possibly creating a new career. As much as she told me how great I would feel, I had to have my own experience. I had to commit on some level. Telling somebody how to do something, or how they will feel about it, is nothing compared to the feeling they get creating an experience for themselves. My mother's dogged perseverance, matched with my commitment to a new possibility, has changed my life forever.

Life has thrown our family some curve balls that I could have never imagined. The opportunity for abundance and stability that my profession, and especially my particular company, provides allowed me to care for our daughter as she struggled with a rare autoimmune disorder. My husband and I were able to stay at the hospital with her and monitor her care as we searched for a diagnosis and treatment. The support of family and friends was critical as we maneuvered through the health care system and tried to provide stability for our younger daughters.

Through this all, my last worry or concern was my income. I didn't have to call clients to cancel jobs. I didn't have to worry if they would find somebody else. I didn't have to be concerned with whether or not I could provide long-term care for my daughter. I was able to just be a mom. In fact, through the efforts of my team, my business actually grew exponentially during that year. This wasn't an overnight success. It was about the foundation—surrounding myself with the right people, asking questions, learning, reading, and listening. REPEAT. I have heard the same information over and over again. It's the stories that stuck with me, personal stories of how someone implemented certain strategies. How did they overcome particular obstacles? Can I relate? One story can change your life.

> *Just like people, negative thoughts and words are detrimental. Replace them. Find a mantra. Write it down, post it, pin it, memorize it. Language is essential to a growing child; it is also a powerful tool as an adult. Positive language is something you can speak to yourself, even when the rest of the world doesn't. It can be the difference between thriving and floundering.*

When fear arises, don't overanalyze it. For me, it can be a powerful motivator to get into motion. It's like that ride at the amusement park, the scary one, that supercolossal roller coaster. It can be the first time you go on it, or the tenth time, because you love it so much. It's fast. It's thrilling. It all hits you at the end of the ride—exciting, scary, wonderful. I want to do it again! You get in the seat and buckle up—you're IN IT. You're ready to go. You just do it. You know when you buckle up, you're not getting out. There's that safety factor. The attendant checked your straps. The buckle is locked. You're ready. Maybe you're doing it with a friend. How great it is to share something this exciting with a friend or loved one sitting right next to you! You are ready! You get what you get out of it. It's the journey! ▣

HEIDI POCHE. *Entrepreneur Heidi Poche, who built up a decorative painting business over the course of ten years, recognized the challenges of balancing business growth and quality family time. When her third daughter was born, she discovered in network marketing the opportunity to create a business from home. Her thirst for knowledge, personal growth, and human connection was the catalyst that gave her the confidence to try something completely unique and different from her previous business. Showing people an opportunity beyond their imagination and providing the tools to turn that opportunity into a reality is the foundation of success for her growing team of more than 14,000 people. Heidi shares this rich insight with you so that not only can you pursue your dreams, you can bring them to the forefront of your life—right now.*

Heidi Poche
heidipoche@me.com

As a Little Girl Thinketh

Monetta Reyes

Suffering is ALWAYS the effect of wrong thought in some direction. It is an indication that the individual is out of harmony with himself, with the Law of his being. The sole and supreme use of suffering is to purify, to burn out all that is useless and impure. There could be no object in burning gold after the dross had been removed, and a perfectly pure and enlightened being could not suffer.

—James Allen

Our beliefs are formed and shaped by our thought life. What we believe creates and shapes our self talk and our lives. As a six-year-old little girl, thirsty from a very busy and fun day at the fair, I repeatedly asked my dad for something to drink—over and over again, whining along the way. I remember it like it was yesterday! I was sitting in the back seat behind my dad, who was soon to drive us the short distance home. The burning in my throat from the cotton candy and the exhaustion from play made me SO THIRSTY! "Please, Daddy, I need some water to drink!"

Daddy, out of exhaustion, I'm sure, reached up, grabbed and twisted the rear-view mirror, and said: "What do want me to do, squeeze water out of here?" What happened next changed my life forever. What I heard next was my own voice, not my father's. The next thought that came to my mind was: "Wow! I must be stupid. How or why would I think that my dad could just pull water out of nowhere? How stupid I must be!" My dad was, I am sure, probably very tired and frustrated from an afternoon with me and my brother. You see, I am slightly ADHD and a wee bit active.

At 52, I can run circles around folks half my age. I never stop unless I'm reading, creating, or sleeping. I'm always asking questions, listening, creating, and finding ways to love on others. My grandmother once said that I would talk to a telephone pole if it would talk back—I hope I'm painting a vivid picture for you. I'm confident that you know me already.

Now, as a grandparent of very active grandchildren, it has occurred to me why they actually choose to "pee" in swimming pools. It was for the same reason that I begged my dad for the water in the parking lot, where there was none. Children do not plan very well for events needed to support their bodies. They go wide open until they are desperate and must STOP having fun in order to manage their vessel. And sometimes, well, it's just too late!

My dad never said I was stupid. I told myself that based on my dad's response to my request for water. That comment I made to myself became my belief. That belief became my life. I would defend the position of stupid, never allowing myself to be challenged academically, especially in front of others. I hid behind smart people in order to appear intelligent, and smart. Oh, yes, I must not forget. Stupid people cannot be beautiful either. I bought into that belief as well.

These are all things that I did to myself. My dad had zero control of MY thought life. This was and has always been my responsibility. I developed and nurtured this defect all on my own. As I grew up and became a teenager, I developed a hate for being corrected. Each time someone would correct me, especially my dad, I would defend my position of stupid. Instead of hearing wisdom I would choose to hear condemnation. (My hearing became distorted because of my belief as well.) So from this was birthed rebellion. Oh my, the things I did! I am fortunate to be alive! I did have a purpose placed within me that went beyond age 20.

My own self-worth was wrapped in the belief that I was stupid! Everything else in life was filtered through that. I never had a diagnosis as a kid regarding ADHD. I knew nothing of it. I just thought that I was a different kind of stupid. It was a stupid that could not sit still or be quiet. I never knew that I was extremely bright and very intelligent but that I learned differently and was bored. So when there was a subject that I had difficulty with I would say to myself,"Oh my, I am not smart enough to learn this. I don't want anyone to know that I can't do this! I won't be able to learn this. I should not think that I could. I won't put myself here because I don't want to fail. I will never ask for help because they cannot find me out!"

That's what we,"me, myself and I,"agreed upon. That's why I did not receive or complete an undergraduate degree. I never had the self-confidence that I could actually do it. The FEAR was bigger than ME. My dream of becoming a dentist was encapsulated, never birthed. I now know that if I had believed in myself, not only would I have made a great dentist, I would have led dentists who are leaders. I would have been on the front lines of research. There is nothing we can do or say that will remove us from our GOD-purposed destiny. The job that I currently have allows me to do exactly this—just not in the way I thought!

My first marriage—I chose a man who I felt had potential but just needed help finding it, whatever"it"was. It was nice to be needed and to be loved by someone so smart! I became focused on helping him to find himself and his purpose. I totally lost myself and my identity in him. I did not believe that I had what it took to be successful in life, but boy he did! He was tall, handsome, and incredibly smart. So I focused on saving him from himself and his defects. I knew how much better my self-worth became when I saw him not wasting his potential. I felt needed and could be helpful. If I could just get him to see what he was capable of, he would have a great job, we would live in a nice house and have a great life with our son.

This spirit of stupid in my life had caused me to become an out-of-control"control freak." I would dictate to him how he would cope with his life instead of trusting God to help us as a family. At age 30, I had a limited formal education; I was living behind the shadow of what my husband could or could not do for us. I was very needy, not to mention my low self-worth and many insecurities. What pressure he must have felt! My marriage was falling apart because I did not love him for who he was, or where he was, but continued to try to change him for what I saw he could be. The pressure of being married to a "controller" became more insanity than he chose to remain in.

My biggest fear, which fueled the controller in me, came true. He left, and I was forced to discover my own strengths and weaknesses. Having a six-year-old son and being over 700 miles from my parents, it was time for me to be responsible for my choices. I made a decision. I would never return home to my parents and burden them with raising my son and providing for us, even if it meant living under the bridge at Gessner and I-10 in Houston. I was about to find out not only how smart, talented, and equipped I really was; I was about to meet a loving and compassionate God, a God who did for me what I could not do for myself.

My life now, after my recovery, is totally different. When my belief changed, my life changed. I live an unbelievable life! It is not perfect—but neither am I. I know that perfection is not part of what will be in this lifetime. It is progress and process that is important! What I now know is that I am not stupid and never have I been. That voice that said "You are different; you're not like everyone else," that resonating fear that was meant to hold me back, is now a brick that I stand on. I have learned that there is nothing that anyone can do or say that will affect me unless I choose to agree with them. What another person says or does has nothing to do with me. It simply shows me where that person is and what they might be dealing with. Everyone has a story.

Nothing is ever what it seems. When I take something personally, it becomes all about me. I become self-focused, and when that happens I am unable to love others where they are. I have discovered that I have a gift, and I am a gift. The God whom I serve is a loving, giving, and selfless God who is perfecting that in me. Remember what I said about not being able to misplace the purpose that God has destined for our lives? You may land in the ditch and off the path. You may find that you have a lot of pain, brokenness, and disappointment because of your choices. There is nothing you can say or do—defects, bad choices, and all—that will remove God's divine purpose from your life. It may be delayed by the choices made, but even then God will supernaturally make and provide all the time you need to accomplish the purpose He has placed within you. I am living proof!

Today, I am grateful for a husband who has taught me about love and forgiveness. He is a mighty man of God with a huge, bigger-than-life servant's heart. He is SO not perfect, and neither am I, but we are both in the process of perfection! Erasmo, we call him Eddie; his name means "to love." What a lucky woman I am! I have three children and three grandchildren who teach me more and more about life and love every day. Loving others where they are and not where I want them and need them to be. It's not about me! It's about empowering those around me, not just my children, to be free to learn from their mistakes and choices—good and bad. It's about loving everyone on purpose. What others do does not determine who they are. It's about building and equipping others in love, encouraging them as they discover and find their own self-worth and purpose, remembering that God is in control, and that we can totally trust Him.

Again, I want to remind you, there is nothing we can do or say to remove what God has purposed in us. It is not what I see with my eyes but what I see with my ever-increasing faith—setting boundaries in love and remaining steadfast, realizing that, until the other person has their epiphany with God, hurt people can hurt people. All of us are consumed with "self" before the "aha." Each young adult and grandchild that we have is perfect where they are; they are God's greatest gifts to many people, not just to my husband and me. I have a great job leading leaders who happen to be dentists. What are the odds of that? I have been blessed with parents who are still alive to see me grow. I have a brother, sisters-in-law, brothers-in-law, nieces, nephews, a great family and friends, and the health to enjoy it. God has so blessed me. My mind is creative and very alert. My heart is truly receptive. God has assigned great potential to me!

I believe that one of the greatest tragedies in this life is having potential and not using it. The sum total of all that is purposed within us is greater than any mistake we could ever make. Mistakes, I have found, are learning opportunities that present themselves as lessons for discovery. These mistakes result in our making better choices. God does not give up! Sometimes, He will even modify the lesson plan in order for us to be able to walk it out. God uses each of us, every second of every day. He is always working. He never sleeps. God is in everything…or He is in nothing.

I have learned over the years that everyone in fact believes there is a God. There is no such thing as an atheist. Atheists are simply angry with God. We are created to be in relationship with Him and with others. When we have that "aha" moment, when we love ourselves as God does, and move beyond our self-love, we become unstoppable. I can tell you that nothing in life worth having is ever easy. Dying to oneself, the "self-love," is a difficult decision, and a decision that cannot be made alone. With the help of God, it can be done all at once or it can happen over time—all one must do is to ask and trust in faith that it WILL be done. I never asked because, frankly, I thought I needed me. My prayer was, "Help me to do unto others as I would have them do unto me." Although a purposeful prayer with great power and benefit, I never saw it as a prayer to put another's need before my own—which would require me to die to Monetta.

While I was dying to myself, I remember my counselor saying to me, "Monetta, at what point are you going to stop ripping off the Band-aid?" What she was telling me was: "Stop it. Heal. Allow yourself to heal. Stop fighting to be heard. Surrender. Let go of the 'what about me,' the pushed-down anger turned inward into depression. LET IT GO. Surrender! Give it up! Lay it down. Sacrifice your life and the desires you have for yourself for that of your friend. Stop pounding your fist and stomping your feet in order to have your own way!"

Nothing else matters in life but loving others. What others do and say about you means absolutely nothing. It is not about you. What another person is saying tells you everything you need to know about them and where they are in life. Stop defending yourself. When people show you who they are, believe them. Another person's behavior has nothing to do with you. You are responsible for your response to others. You must first love yourself—selflessly. You cannot give away something you do not have.

The battle begins, in our mind, with our thinking. Bad thoughts can never produce good. Good thoughts can never produce bad. Do you have a lie that you have made your belief around which you have built your life? If so, how much has it cost you, your family and friends, and will you allow it to cost you your future?

Your beliefs become your thoughts,
Your thoughts become your words,
Your words become your actions,
Your actions become your habits,
Your habits become your values,
Your values become your destiny.

—Mahatma Gandi

MONETTA REYES *grew up in Alabama where she attended the University of Alabama in Birmingham. She graduated with honors from both Dental Assisting and Dental Hygiene programs. Monetta has served dentistry for 35 years as instructor, dental hygienist, dental assistant, receptionist, treatment counselor, office administrator, dental office designer, dental sales representative, coach, speaker, consultant, and author. She has traveled the world exploring best practices, and her work reflects this. Her success has been featured in publications such as* Dental Economics, Dentaltown, *and* Patterson Today. *Monetta is currently employed by Patterson companies as a trusted advisor to dentists and the teams that support them. She designs, builds, and develops phenomenal dental practices, specializing in new startups, acquisitions, and reinventions, as well as leading and equipping others to fulfill their purpose.*

Monetta Reyes is a beautiful daughter, sister, wife, mother, grandmother, aunt, niece, cousin, sister-in-law, employee, coworker, colleague, and friend. Her wisdom and life experiences bring hope, joy, and clarity to all who know and trust her. Her passion is inspiringly contagious and makes an impact and a difference in the lives of others.

Monetta Reyes
ardentimpact@gmail.com
monettareyes.com
monettareyes.net

9:08 a.m. March 10th, 1988
Matt Rush

It was a hot, sultry, March afternoon, a day unlike anything that we're accustomed to in March on the high plains of Eastern New Mexico—because it was completely still. Occasionally, you could feel a slight wisp of a breeze kiss your cheek just enough to make you appreciate the slight, instantaneous relief it brought. It was one of those spring days that made you acutely aware that the "really" hot days of summer were marching forward.

I was in the eighth grade, and all I had on my mind was spring break; it was coming, and I wished we could go on vacation. BUT, I knew dad was going to make us work the entire break on the farm.

On this particular day, I was hunkered down in the passenger seat as dad drove us down the dry, dusty county road in his 1969, filthy, dirty, old, work pickup. Originally, it was two-tone red and white, but those colors had faded years ago! And because of a mishap with a tractor, the bed of that "thing" had been demolished. So dad found a used solid-white pickup bed at a wrecking yard—and the work pickup was back in service! NOW, it was two-tone red and white AND white. A classic!

The only air conditioning that pickup had ever seen was the 255 kind—you know, two windows down and at least 55 miles per hour. We always hoped that dad wouldn't open those little side windows that all those old pickups had because with all the dirt that was built up on the dash from being on the farm, it was going to create a flashback to the Dust Bowl Days! Not to mention that you had to frantically try to anchor down that mass of papers and "stuff" that was mounded up across the dash. So, not only was I hunkered down in that embarrassing hunk of dirty, farm-truck metal, I was also sweating. Ugh! No power steering. Standard transmission. AM radio only—the one with dials. KFYO was the only station we could get—except sometimes at night you could pick up WBAP out of Fort Worth or maybe KVOO out of Shreveport/Bossier City. Of course, you really just tried making out the words through the classic AM radio static. I was as miserable as any eighth grader could be.

As kids, my older brother Wayne and my younger sister Janie and I were embarrassed to be seen even standing close to that old pickup, much less having to ride somewhere in it. For me, there was just NO WAY in the world that an eighth grader could look cool when that's all you had to work with. I always prayed that I wouldn't see anyone I knew because, after all, as an eighth grader, image was becoming everything.

This story, however, isn't one of those "back in my day I walked uphill both ways" stories. What was about to happen that day on that hot, dusty, dirt road would take away any worry I had about being seen in that pickup. My life was about to change forever.

That morning, after my older brother, my younger sister, and I had left for school, Dad left the farm and went to town. On his way back to the farm he stopped at the school and checked me out early so that I could go help him repair a broken piece of farm equipment. He was doing a farming job for a neighboring farmer who lived further south of our house. I remember exactly where the field was that he was working in and where we were headed. It was on a dirt road that goes from downtown Lingo, New Mexico, straight across to what we called the Lovington Highway. From our house you just went south down some really bad dirt roads, past the old Doke place, past Wayne and Lella Victor's house, and then you turned back east at the old Lot place, crossed two cattle guards, opened one gate, and the field was on the south side of the county road.

I don't remember what kind of farm work we were doing down there, but, whatever it was, I'm sure I would have rather stayed in school.

We were on our way back to the house, and I noticed that dad was going even slower than usual—he didn't even have to shift down to cross the cattle guards. After what seemed like hours, with no words being spoken at all, he reached up on the dash and handed me something that would change my life forever. It was a set of papers, the formal kind that you can just glance at and tell they are important. At the top of the page was a raised seal, the kind of seal that is made when you insert the paper into a device and squeeze together firmly so it forms a lasting impression into the very paper itself.

As soon as I saw it, I knew. I knew what those papers were. The only thing dad said was, "It's over." My parents were no longer married.

It had been a year in coming. I can even remember when mom came in one night and told us kids that she was moving out. She walked around the corner of the kitchen into the living room, sat down on the end of the couch, and said she had something she had to tell us. She was wearing purple slacks and a matching blouse with flowers on it. Wayne, Janie and I were sitting on the floor in the living room folding the whites that had just finished drying. Janie was on the floor leaning against the couch and Wayne and I were lying in front of the old panel ray heater. She told us that she and my dad just didn't love each other anymore, and she was going to be moving out.

Through tears and a horrific, sick, gnawing in my stomach, I choked out the inevitable question, "Are you and dad getting a divorce?" I don't remember if she said yes, no, or probably. I just remember she told us that no matter what happened between her and our dad that she loved us so very much.

That was in February. It was cold. There was snow on the ground. I don't know where dad had gone that night, but knowing what was going on in that living room, I'm sure it was an incredibly cold and lonely place. I also cannot imagine what it was like for mom to have to come in and tell us what was happening. It was awful—for all of us.

I lay with my stomach on the floor and cried. My brother Wayne tried to comfort me by rubbing his hand gently on my back, but I shrugged it away. I shrugged it away the way someone does when at that moment they don't want anyone in the world to touch them. That made him mad. He was only trying to help ease my pain and probably his too. I didn't care, I was hurt. I was changed forever.

The year after that February conversation had been a long one. Dad and mom both seemed to be able to tell me things that were going on. On several occasions dad would even tell me that we needed to go for a ride—in that pickup, of course. But as I held my parents' divorce papers in my hand on that dry, dusty, hot day, I know that old pickup kept moving but, everything in my world stopped. The words, "It's over," echoed through my head as I stared at those papers. At the top of the front page, in the middle of the mark that the raised seal had left, something was written that from that moment on I swore I would never forget. It was the exact hour, minute, and day that my mom and dad's marriage no longer existed.

It was final.

It was over.

It was finished.

9:08 a.m., March 10, 1988.

At that very instant, that moment in time, I swore I would never forget, because, so help me God, I never wanted to go through that again.

I know some of you have experienced the pains of divorce, and I dare say that every one of us has been touched by it. And you may be thinking, "Great! The single guy is going to give us marital advice!"

I am not at all qualified to give marital advice. What I want to talk about is change. I share the story of my parents' divorce with you, having shared it with only a few, small groups of people before, because it was the biggest "CHANGE" I have ever personally experienced.

Each and every one of us could name something that has changed us. Like me, it may have been a divorce. For you, it may have been the death of a husband, a wife, a child, or a dear friend. Maybe you lost your home or your job. Maybe you were forced to change jobs or had a great financial disaster. Was your change a move or the loss of someone to a move? Maybe something happened when you were in school and it rocked your very foundation. We certainly remember the negative changes that hit us. Hopefully, yours was a good change. A great, positive one!

Regardless, we have all experienced some type of change. And we have all heard the comment that everything is changing, or everything has changed and nothing remains the same. Think back on the last week, the last month, the last year. Was it five or ten years ago that a change affected you? Whatever it was, there have been COUNTLESS changes in all our lives. Some changes we don't even remember. Yet some changes scar us for life, and we can never forget.

Some changes force us to become a better person, a different person. With all the changes that impact our lives, what do most of us say about change? Most of us will quickly say that we HATE change. We want things to stay the same. We want things to stay the way we like them. We want to stay comfortable. We want everyone to get along; we don't want anyone to have to make those tough decisions in life; and we don't ever want to let loved ones go—we don't like change!

However, change isn't necessarily bad, is it? Absolutely not! In fact, as a Christian, even the worst of changes can be turned into a positive. In the Scriptures we read in Romans 8:28 (NIV): "All things work together toward the good for those that love the Lord." Of course, here on this earthly sojourn, we may never know what the good is or was. We may have to work like the dickens to find good in some of the changes in our lives. But, regardless of that fact, it is a fact that we are going to experience change.

For example, what do they say about time? It never stands still. It's always changing. What is said of youth? Youth is fleeting. What does the Bible say in James 4:14 about life? "Life is a vapor that appears for a little

124

while then vanishes away."

As a leader do we have to change? Do we need to change? Are we where we need to be? Have we reached our full potential?

Socrates said,"The secret of change is to focus all of your energy, not on fighting the old, but on building the new." All too often we live life moving forward at breakneck speed while looking back. Several years ago, my friend James Johnson and I put together a workbook on leadership. In the introduction we started with the following quote from Henry Ford: "No one built a reputation based upon what they were going to do." In other words, YOU are going to have to do something. YOU are going to have to change.

If you walk into any bookstore, the one thing that you are assured to find is row after row of books on leadership; there are literally THOU-SANDS! And now you are holding one more. And why are there so many books on leadership? For starters, look behind you. How many people are following you? Maybe we should ask: "Are there as many people following you as there should be?" Very rarely is our rear-view mirror operating at full capacity.

You already know the theories and principles of leadership. In fact, if you are like most people who aspire to be better leaders, you have stacks of books on the subject. Why? Because you want to change, you know you need to change, and in return you want to become better. Most people just want an aspirin that will make them all better right now. However, it's not long until life hits hard again, and, if you are not care-ful, you slip right back where you were.

It does not matter how many leadership books you read or seminars you attend; they will not CHANGE you unless YOU put the applications to work in your everyday leadership practice. Don't forget, you've got to get out there and BUILD that reputation! You have to change.

DEVOTIONAL THOUGHTS:

Now for the big question: Do you think God likes change? Consider the following:

Matthew 18:3:"I tell you the truth, unless you CHANGE

and become like little children, you will never enter the kingdom of heaven."

When Samuel is anointing Saul what does he say to Saul? In 1 Samuel 10.6 we read: "The spirit of the Lord will come upon you and you will be changed into a different person."

And what do we read in Ecclesiastes 3? Everything has its time—everything is going to change.

1 Corinthians 15:50–58 states: "I declare to you, brothers and sisters, that flesh and blood cannot inherit the kingdom of God, nor does the perishable inherit the imperishable. Listen, I tell you a mystery: We will not all sleep, but we will all be changed—in a flash, in the twinkling of an eye, at the last trumpet. For the trumpet will sound, the dead will be raised imperishable, and we will all be CHANGED. For the perishable must clothe itself with the imperishable, and the mortal with immortality. When the perishable has been clothed with the imperishable, and the mortal with immortality, then the saying that is written will come true: 'Death has been swallowed up in victory.'"

"Where, O death, is your victory? Where, O death, is your sting?" The sting of death is sin, and the power of sin is the law. But thanks be to God! He gives us the victory through our Lord Jesus Christ. Therefore, my dear brothers and sisters, stand firm. Let nothing move you. Always give yourselves fully to the work of the Lord, because you know that your labor in the Lord is not in vain."

What's the whole gospel of Christ about? What was the reason that the LIVING GOD JEHOVAH sent his only son to die?

Why? So that we might, maybe, possibly…change. So that we could then be made like him. See Philippians 3:12–21.

I'll confess here. Do you know what one of my problems is? I don't think I've changed enough. Hebrews, chapter 5, has really hit home with me. Starting with the second half of verse 11 and continuing through verse 14, it states:"…we have much to say, and it is hard to explain, since you have become dull of hearing. For though by this time you ought to be teachers, you have need again for someone to teach you the elementary principles of the oracles of God, and you have come to need milk and not solid food. For everyone who partakes only of milk is not accustomed to the word of righteousness, for he is a babe. But solid food is for the mature, who because of practice have their senses trained to discern good and evil."

Sometimes I feel as if my spiritual life might still find me slipping back to a bottle of milk. But maybe that's just me. We all need to experience change.

However, in all this changing, good, bad or otherwise, what one thing do we know beyond the shadow of ANY doubt? Let's end it on a HIGH note.

Hebrews 13.5:"Because God has said, 'Never will I leave you; never will I forsake you.' So we say with confidence, 'The Lord is my helper; I will not be afraid. What can man do to me?'" Remember your leaders, who spoke the words of God to you. Consider the outcome of their way of life and imitate their faith. Verse 8:"JESUS IS THE SAME YESTERDAY AND TODAY AND FOREVER."

James 1:17: "Every good and perfect gift is from above, coming down from the Father of the heavenly lights, who does not change like the shifting shadows."

Hebrews 4:16: "Let us therefore draw near, with confidence, to the throne of grace, that we may receive mercy and may find the grace to help in time of need."

No matter what changes take place here in our lives, WE KNOW that… he has set our feet on a rock and gave us a firm place to stand (Psalm 40:2). And Psalm 61:2 states:"From the ends of the earth I call to you, I call as my heart grows faint; lead me to the rock that is higher than I."

Is he your ROCK, your ANCHOR that holds within the gale? If not, why? If you thought you had changed but deep down you know you haven't, do it because we are talking about YOU and the eternity YOU are going to spend in heaven or hell.

How many of YOU know that YOU can do something in the next week to make your life worse?

How many of YOU know that YOU can do something in the next week to make your life better?

We KNOW how to change our lives for the better.

We KNOW who the only one is who can help us truly change for the better.

And, when we change for Him, we KNOW where we will spend eternity! ▓

MATT RUSH *is the fourth generation in his family to be a New Mexico farmer and cattle rancher. To support his "farm habit," Rush travels the country as a professional speaker conducting leadership and motivational seminars. He has served as the CEO of the New Mexico Farm Bureau and is past president of the Ethos Leadership Group; he is also a member of the New Mexico State Fair Commission and the New Mexico Natural Lands Protection Committee and has served on the American Farm Bureau's Foundation for Agriculture board of directors and the Berean Children's Home board of directors. In addition, Rush was a member of the first class to become Ziglar Legacy Certified Trainers with the Zig Ziglar Corporation.*

Mr. Rush has won state and national awards for his public speaking and co-authored a book on leadership entitled, Why Is No One Following Me? *He has been quoted in the* Bloomberg Business Weekly, *as well as on* NPR, PBS, *and the* ABC News. *Matt is passionate about his values, helping others, and the future for our next generation.*

Matt Rush
matt@mattrush.net
575-760-7874

15

A Chaplain for All Seasons
Veronica Sites

When my mentor has something I need to hear to obtain growth, I allow myself to listen with love, trusting that she is also my friend. In that precious moment, a chaplain can become a friend for life, the kind of friend who cares for you and who desires the very best for you, always and in all ways. Friendship with a chaplain provides a friend who is loyal to love at all times, including the kind of love that may be painful to hear at first—the truth as a form of "tough love." Speaking the truth in love may even be a bit painful for the chaplain to share, but the chaplain does so anyway to encourage and challenge us. If we aren't challenged, then we can't change. My role as a chaplain is to reach out to others as a friend.

Prior to becoming a chaplain, I did not know the full scope of a chaplain's roles and responsibilities, other than what I knew from limited experiences with military and law enforcement chaplains. I could only draw from an experience I had when a chaplain of my dad's unit was assigned to help my family through uncertain days following a shooting.

The field of chaplaincy covers a multitude of environments where chaplains are greatly needed, such as hospitals, corporations, the community of law enforcement and first responders, airports, as well as part of disaster relief. When I was in grad school, I was approached by a professor to consider a career as a chaplain. I quickly dismissed the idea. It was such a foreign concept to me. However, the seed was planted. Over time, I became intrigued; and yet I felt somewhat intimidated and, in a way, almost frightened. Why me? My mentor saw something in me that I had yet to even ponder.

LEARNING TO LISTEN

Have you ever wondered why things happen—especially to you? Have you considered the possibility of a bigger picture with a greater purpose than what the perspective of a moment or season in life provides? In hindsight it is much easier to understand the purpose. But in the moment, thoughts and emotions can cloud our mind and perspective. That was my initial bewilderment at the suggestion that I pursue chaplaincy. Nonetheless, I decided to give due diligence to the possibility, and began my quest learning about the role of a corporate chaplain.

When I was initially approached about such a career, it was suggested that I consider working in the corporate world. My collective experiences as a missionary and my heart for helping others—combined with the knowledge that bilingual women were in high demand for chaplains in the workplace—further drove the point home that my "home" is where my heart is. And, even still, I pushed the thought away. While a career as a corporate chaplain sounded interesting, I did not think it was for me.

A couple of years after dismissing the possibility of navigating toward the unknown, my curiosity, my need for employment, and to employ my degree, I pursued a job as a corporate chaplain. Throughout the process, my eager curiosity was met with thoughts wrangling in an inner debate and concluding in the obvious: I had no business considering a career in such an esteemed profession, one that far exceeded a simple call to ministry. Essentially, I was stuck in the mindset of equating a chaplain with the military. I am familiar with the military and law enforcement world, as I have many relatives in both. But the world of "Corporate America" was still a foreign concept to me.

One interview and a single defining decision later, I finally discovered my niche. During my initial years of service, I discovered that I was definitely wired for chaplaincy. My life's experience and education have equipped me powerfully to serve as a confidant, a "connector of resources," and a natural networker to counsel when solicited. I discovered my ability to listen and to love every single person with whom I come in contact. I learned the depth of compassion and care I have for my fellow man. Now, more than ever, I appreciate what I have learned by considering a mentor's perspective.

Plans fail for lack of counsel, but with many advisors they succeed. A person finds joy in giving a great reply—and how good is a timely word (Proverbs 15:22–23). And, to humans belong the plans of the heart, but from the Lord comes the proper answer of the tongue (Proverbs 16:1).

I did not know that accepting the job was not only divine obedience, it was the beginning of embracing my life's purpose. Becoming a chaplain came to be a careful work of art in refining integrity and authenticity with a deep heart that at times is very familiar with experiences from which to draw upon to help others. When I first learned that the job description entailed assistance from the womb to the tomb, I had one hesitancy—death notifications. I was licensed and commissioned to commence.

DREAD AND DISCOVERY

I could anticipate death notifications and honestly dreaded it. I hoped that would not come for a long time. Five days on the job I was called to muster academics and natural abilities I did not know I possessed: I had to deliver a death notification. You don't learn how to give notifications in seminary. I will never forget the three young girls I notified that their dad was dead. Practicum is learning by immersion. No amount of education could have prepared me for that moment. Providentially, God and life's experience had.

In an instant, a veil was lifted to reveal why I had come through traumatic events in my life. I was in similar shoes once, and thoughts of how I would rather have been told gave me the empathy they and

I needed. Since then, I seldom ask why something happens to me. I have learned instead to ask, "What difference is this going to make so that I can help others?" I cherish the opportunity to inspire others by what I have learned in overcoming various trials. Chaplaincy requires more listening to others than me talking. My compassion and empathy to respond to some extreme situations are by choice, and today I serve as a volunteer chaplain. It is my network skills that energize our income—but that is another story.

It did not take long for me to learn a life lesson that is not often considered. I came to realize that in life every person is in one of three places: entering, coming out of, or in the midst of a crisis. Education teaches and prepares theory and encourages planned or mapped-out courses of action or reaction. The school of proverbial hard knocks approaches learning at the practical level. There is a huge difference between teaching and learning. I will interject as well that those with the mind-set that "those who can do, and those who cannot teach" is wrong! The impact of one's gifts and skills should be used wherever fruit is produced. In either case, the educator bears fruit, and others around can recognize abilities, sometimes even before the skilled or gifted individual can.

Circumstances can chisel into a masterpiece any vessel willing to be molded, broken, and reset to be a unique work of art with beautiful value in this world. On the other hand, such lessons are more caught than taught. Beauty is not always in the eyes of the beholder. Sometimes it takes the vision of what someone else sees to consider possibilities. Learning is attained by gained perspective. One willing to learn will learn. One done with education is unteachable and limited in realizing their full potential personally and will continue unsatisfied or unsettled because they are not fulfilling their purpose in the world.

Helen Keller could not see or hear, but her amazing teacher and lifelong mentor Anne Sullivan saw potential. Anne heard compassion cry out in her heart so much so that she believed in and for Helen until Helen's perspective changed. Anne allowed her education and life experience to make a difference. She believed more for Helen until Helen embraced the same belief. Helen was not only taught, she caught the vision of her true potential. A blind and deaf little girl flourished and came to believe in herself to the end that Helen Adams Keller became an American author, political activist, and lecturer. She was the first deaf and blind person to earn a Bachelor of Arts degree.

Allow me to ask you: What are you not seeing, and what have you not heard in realizing your potential? It could be closing your eyes or muting what others have encouraged or observed as your abilities. Friend, do yourself and the world a favor and embrace your potential. The world needs you!

LIFE LEARNING

I believe there is no hurt that comes into our lives that will not later be used to help others in their seasons of trial. I believe too, after years of Bible college and seminary and witness to so many debates over theological positions, that the theory of theology some-times becomes a blindfold to the reason anyone responds to a call to minister. My education equipped me to critique every thought, book, theological stance in print and has served my intellect well. Higher education prepared me academically and through required practicums brought me to graduation. Nonetheless, had I not remained a student beyond degrees earned, I could not have reached greater depth of growth and intimacy in my relationship with my Lord Jesus and those he loves. He is ever revealing himself and furthering my learning so that I can be what and who I am today. Life is not defined by one's career, brand, or job, even if it is the highest calling—parenthood. Each individual has purpose and potential beyond any role assumed. Likewise, we also have hang-ups that squelch who we allow ourselves to become.

I do not know your story, and no doubt it is still being written, but you have the ability to effect change in how your life's story ends. Life is a series of seasons. There are seasons of joy, pain, sorrow, life, death, and sickness. Health and healing come when chosen. The psalmist imparts truth from your Creator when he says to everything there is a season.

In my adolescence I became familiar with the life of law enforcement families, and it never occurred to me then; but, in hindsight, I recall that a chaplain aided our family in a very difficult season. Healing is a unique season; it is not easy, and it takes time. Healing is a choice in matters of the heart, hopes deferred, or shattered dreams. Healing is possible, and I am here to encourage, empower, and equip people to move forward from tragedy to triumph. Traumatic circumstances can be opportunities for triumphant transformation. Life events shape us, and how we weather the random storms of life either makes or breaks us—either way, healing and growth are optional. Please choose healing.

BRIGHT FUTURE

I volunteer with Victim Relief Ministries and organizations that serve first responders and victims of crime. I also deploy as part of disaster relief and crisis management teams when necessary. My greatest joy is to network in community and the world at large. There is no one we cannot impact when we seek where we can add value.

We live in a hurting world that needs the hope I bring to the marketplace. Through cultivating relationships, speaking and mentoring individuals, I carry out my mission. My passion is to impact community one life at a time. I know I cannot change the world. One thing I can do is invest in impacting the world of one person at a time, and exponentially that can make a world of difference. My role as chaplain is to be authentic and transparent, and to serve to impact lives. In life, and through all I have gained the privilege to do in serving others, I have repeatedly observed and counseled hurt people, and this remains true: hurt people hurt people, and free people free people. Or, put another way, I have healed and overcome many tragedies, and I live free from the impact of depression and discouragement, doubt and resentment. I am forgiven and free; therefore, it is my passion to bring hope and light to dark places. A chaplain goes to where people are, which could be to any location in any season of life transition. ■

 VERONICA SITES *is a Ziglar Legacy Certified Trainer and certified in Critical Incident Stress Management. As a growth coach, facilitating healthy personal development is her passion. She is founder of Sites Edutainment and Bridge The Gap Academy where equipping individuals starts with goal-setting and effecting action plans as part of overcoming challenges in life and career. Stress management requires skill and compassion to help others progress healthily at emotional, psychological, and physical levels of care following traumatic events. Knowledge of business empowers understanding the need for varied levels of crisis intervention from injury or death in the workplace to caring for employees and family members as a support system and resource. Those who value the health and wellness of employees know the impact this has in productivity and sustainable revenue in business.*

Veronica imparts hope at the practical level as she connects with an audience. She addresses the following: My Traumatic Transformation, Stopping Depression's Downward Spiral, Home Business Requires Owner Operation, Goal Plan Systems Requires a Board. Her mission: Impacting Community One Life at a Time.

Veronica Sites
info@chaplainveronica.com
972-489-9476.
www.chaplainveronica.com

16

Nothing Changes
If Nothing Changes
Niccole Smith

I remember the day my entire life shifted. I believe anyone who has made a significant change or decision does. I was 27 years old, a mommy of a beautiful three-year-old little girl, and a devoted, dutiful wife. I say dutiful because I did everything a wife is SUPPOSED to do. Stand by your man…no matter what. Until that very day….

Sitting at his computer, realizing I was still battling the same issues nearly seven and a half years after the first time, a voice, a very strong, bold, powerful voice, spoke to me. I believe it was God's voice. Others may call it their inner voice. Call it what you will, either way, it spoke. It was very clear, and it said to me, "You are in exactly the same place today as you were over seven years ago, and if you stay, if you do not change something now, in another seven years you will be in exactly the same place you are today."

My first thought was, "Is this all there is? Is this my purpose?" To stay stagnant? To not grow? Is this really how I am supposed to spend my life?

We had real issues in the marriage—not the normal "he didn't put the toilet paper on the roll" issues—REAL issues. Beginning six months into the marriage I knew I was in pretty deep, but, as most women do, I held on to the fairy tale of who I thought we could be—not who we really were.

Along with the behaviors I allowed with that fairy tale, I was slowly realizing what the behaviors I had allowed thus far were really saying about me, about who I believed I was, about what I believed I was worth. Each time I ignored the problem, or let it go, I lost a little part of me. A little sparkle in my eye began to dull. My proverbial cup was slowly evaporating, situation by situation.

Peace at any price was not cheap. It actually had quite a price tag: It cost me my self-worth. The lack of that belief in myself was holding me back—holding me back as a woman, as a mom, and as the person I am meant to be. I lost my real value, and if I didn't value myself how on earth could I teach my daughter to be valued?

The world I had grown up in was not one of positive influences or affirmations. I knew people scored goals but not that they set them. I didn't know motivational speakers or books on self-improvement even existed. I thought the life I was living was exactly what it was supposed to be. All those wonderful things only existed in the movies. They were meant for other people. I wasn't deserving of all things great, respectful, and honorable. Don't misunderstand me, I have always been a positive person, whatever the situation, but in this particular situation, I thought, "This is as good as it gets. I made my bed and I must sleep in it."

Then, I started to want things to be better. I wanted more. I wanted to feel better. I wanted to show my daughter what a healthy life looked like. I wanted her to know security as I had not known it. I no longer wanted to feel the way I did every day—the constant insecurity, the inner conflict, the anquish, the overwhelming feeling of self-doubt, and the judgment that I was weak. I wanted it all gone, but I could not find the strength. I wanted a heart change. I needed a heart change.

I started to think about what I wanted in a marriage, in a partner, and a father for my daughter. I thought of what I wanted in life. I thought of what I wanted for my daughter. I actually began to picture the life I WANTED to live. I started to surround myself with people who already had marriages like what I envisioned, people who had morals and beliefs that were similar. As hard as it was, I was going to get rid of the toxicity in my life.

It was a slow process at first because it does come with guilt. It comes with the "Who do I think I am?" thoughts. But it is absolutely necessary. Just as addicts must let go of all of the friends who use with them, I believe that when you are trying to leave a close, toxic relationship you must rid yourself of all toxicity.

I think most of us who are in that situation are somewhat addicted to it. It is a process. I had actually tried to leave the marriage two times prior. The final time was after a situation in which my sweet three-year-old saw me crying after an ugly phone call one afternoon. She put her tiny little three-year-old hands on my cheeks, held my face, and said, "I don't like when my daddy makes you cry." That was one of many red flags for me. However, I still hung onto the white-picket-fence fairy tale.

I did move out into my own apartment, but we still tried to work on our marriage. In other words, I still allowed my sparkle to dull. I still believed the fantasy. So there I was, separated, still dating my husband, and convincing myself that I am deserving of all I was getting. I vividly remember one day actually saying out loud while I was completely alone, "You got yourself here; you'd better stay." But I was so wrong. I knew if I was unhappy, that meant there was more. I clearly wanted more, or I wouldn't be so unhappy. I wasn't even content. I wasn't living—I was existing. The only way things would change was if things changed.

On that day at that computer, when the voice spoke, instantly, all the pain, the anguish, indecisiveness, inner conflict, self-doubt, sadness, and weakness left my body. I stood taller and stronger and more confident than I had in years. Instantly, the world had literally been lifted from my shoulders. My heart had changed. Everything was so clear that even the air felt fresher. I stood up, turned off the computer, and gathered a few of my things from around the apartment. I took his apartment key off my key ring, and I set it on the kitchen counter. I didn't even realize I was smiling until I passed the mirror on the way out the door. I took a deep breath, and I walked away. I never had any doubt about my decision after that day.

The effects, however, took a little longer to change. You see, it takes quite a while to reprogram yourself, your thoughts, and your beliefs, to comprehend that all those things, all those behaviors that felt normal all those years, did not mean what you thought. Jealousy to me equaled love. If he was angry and jealous, that meant he loved me so much he was afraid to lose me. THIS mentality was the hardest thing for me to change because that was where I felt worthy—and maybe most people do. The more you think you are loved, the more you think you are worth. It was crucial for me to be honest with myself about the toxic behaviors I was "addicted" to, and that was the biggest challenge. This was the belief system I had.

My next relationship proved to me how addictive those toxic behaviors were. There was a situation when I was supposed to meet with my new, amazing, kind man for a late date after he was off work. He was going to be at work quite a while, so I decided to have an early dinner with some friends from work, something that would have been frowned upon in my previous marriage. Of course, like women do, we went beyond the time I had anticipated, so I called to let him know I was now finished and apologized profusely for being late. I had prepared myself for what would have happened to me in the past. He was actually stuck at work; he was incredibly sweet and asked if I had a good time. This was unbelievably confusing to me. I thought, "He isn't mad or jealous or accusing me of anything—he doesn't care. He doesn't love me."

That statement, that thought, changed my life. Why? Because it changed the cycle! I realized that the response I had received is what happens in normal healthy relationships. I had gotten out of an unhealthy relationship, so why would I want to be back into anything that resembled it? If I was going to truly change I had to redefine "healthy" and "unhealthy." From that point on, I made daily positive talk a habit. "I AM BEAUTIFUL AND I AM WORTH IT" became my mantra. And soon, I started to believe it.

It is truly amazing how a few simple, positive words every day can literally change your life. I began to change internally. I was a better mother almost instantly after the day I left my key on that counter. I had an inner strength that I never knew existed. In every area of my life I realized that conflict comes only when you truly know a decision has to be made and you don't want to make it. You already know the answer—you just don't want to hear it. I didn't want to admit that I had made mistake, that I had kept my beautiful little girl in an unhealthy environment for longer than necessary. In trying not to "run" from problems, I stayed far too long. I had hoped for so long that I could keep the family unit together.

The truth is, you just know. You know deep down. No matter how hard you try to convince yourself otherwise, you know. Shame, fear, and comfort keep you from making the decision. I became comfortable in dysfunction. I became functional in dysfunction. At least I always knew what to expect if I stayed where I was. Becoming a single mom—now THAT was scary! But it really wasn't. It was liberating. It was freeing. It was beautiful. It was me. The scariest, most trying time in my life was the most beautiful.

It is so important to realize, in most situations, you have the power already in you. You already have the strength. The challenge is in learning and knowing how to gather it. From the most trying time, I have received the best gifts of my life. I have the most incredible, now 14-year-old daughter, and I moved to Texas because of that previous marriage.

Today am still with that amazing, kind man who taught me that I am worthy of love and respect, and his beautiful 16-year-old daughter (my gift with purchase). We own our dream home, I am the owner of my own business, and I now have a partner who pushes me to be the best me that I can be. I now have security, I now have self-worth, and I have found my sparkle.

Everybody has a past. You are living your present. But you can CHANGE your future. With a little courage, self-awareness, and DESIRE for improvement, you can literally change anything. The decision, the power, the choice is in you to have the life you want. Until you confront yourself with brutal, sweet honesty, nothing changes if nothing changes. ▪

 NICCOLE SMITH, *founder and owner of Wine & ReDesign is an energetic, free spirited entrepeneur and business owner. Originally from Brigham City, Utah, a small one-high-school town, she knows about humble beginnings and that God always has a plan. The oldest of three children and raised by a loving single mother, Niccole has personally had to overcome poverty and dysfunction in* her early years and then again later in life. After moving to Texas in 2002 and leaving an unhealthy marriage, Niccole has found love, happiness, and her passion. She has always had an affinity for "all things pretty" at her core. From the start, she has had a God-given talent for home design. She worked as a designer and visual merchandiser for a high-end furniture company for many years and recently launched her own company, Wine & ReDesign. This self-starter has worked hard to bring beauty and balance into the lives of others and has a deep passion for encouraging positivity and wellness in the hearts of women facing adversity. She has a wide variety of professional experiences, all of which have two things in common: helping others become the best they can be and beauty in one form or another.

Niccole's personal experience, her passion for people, and her pure heart have given her the inner strength and desire to help other women find the strength they need to become the best they can be. Friends and loved ones would describe her as very energetic, creative, attentive, and, most of all, affectionate. She currently lives in McKinney, Texas, and loves decorating, crafting, socializing, meeting new people, eating, cooking, party planning, volunteering, and, especially, spending time with her fiancé, their fourteen-year-old and sixteen-year-old daughters, and their three dogs.

Niccole Smith
Wineandredesign@yahoo.com
Niccoleasa@yahoo.com
972-693-4920

17

Don't Let Your Losses Define You
Deanna Sullivan

When I told my dear friend Paul that I wanted to be a motivational speaker, he replied, "Deanna, normally motivational speakers have overcome some tragedy, some loss in their lives. You have a great life. You appear to be very successful. How can you offer people words of encouragement if you haven't lost anything?"

Now to be fair, I haven't lost a limb or an organ and my body isn't disfigured. I had both my parents growing up and they weren't alcoholics or drug addicts. While we were poor, we had food to eat and clothes to wear. But Paul did have a point. Most motivational speakers do have a handicap or they've made some incredible accomplishment or are just famous people. I had none of those. But I had suffered loss in my life that I thought people could relate to so I began telling my story.

Over ten years ago, my wonderful mother was diagnosed with multiple myeloma, a very painful cancer. She had been terribly ill and bedridden, so we were relieved to discover the cause, especially when we were told it was treatable. We didn't learn until later that treatable doesn't mean curable. The doctors in Abilene did as much as they could the first year; she had chemo and radiation and was able to walk again. But the doctors felt she needed to go to the MD Anderson cancer specialists in Houston to further improve. Fortunately, my husband and I were living in Houston, so she and Daddy could stay with us. Every morning when we drove her to the hospital, she would get out of the car with this amazing look on her face. That memory is etched in my mind. She had a look of hope, determination, fear, and faith—faith in us, faith in the doctors, and most importantly faith in God.

After the first month's stay, Mother and Daddy would come to Houston periodically, and she seemed to be getting better or at least stabilized. In fact, during the last visit, we had even gone to a couple of stores and shopped and laughed. My friends had recommended taking some time off to spend with her. But I had a demanding career and thought she was doing better, so I didn't heed their advice.

Just a couple of weeks after the last visit we got a call saying that she was feeling very ill and her doctor told her to fly back to Houston immediately. My husband picked them up at the airport and called to let me know that she looked really bad. That was not what I wanted to hear.

So I took them to the hospital early the next morning. The doctor tested her and said that the cancer had come back—and with a vengeance. He gave her two choices. She could try chemo, but because the cancer had spread so much he wasn't hopeful. Or she could do hospice for what was left of her time. I was blown away. How could this be happening? Just two weeks earlier we had laughed and smiled. How could she have gone down so quickly? My mother was a fighter and wanted to try, so we proceeded to check her into the hospital and get her prepped for chemo the next day.

Ironically, I had a very important meeting that afternoon which I was going to have to cancel. My husband and I had an appointment with a marriage counselor which we'd told no one about. Obviously, my mother took priority, but I had been looking forward to this session. I knew we needed a third-party perspective on our situation as we had been taking each other for granted—well, I knew I had him and felt he had me too. My job required me to travel extensively, as did his, so when we were home neither wanted to focus on household duties. We wanted to go out and play golf and have fun. He wanted kids and we hadn't been successful. I had a blossoming career as a partner with Arthur Andersen, so I was fulfilled by my work and often spent long hours on the job.

As you can surmise, long hours at work don't always make for a successful marriage. He wanted me home more and blamed the partnership for part of our stress. I felt I had to handle everything around the house as well as my full-time job (a common complaint from working wives, I understand). So we needed this counseling and a reenergizing of our marriage—but it wasn't going to happen that Friday afternoon.

It took the rest of the day to find a room and get ready for the chemo. Mother was exhausted, and I was too. The next few days seemed to fly by. We thought that the chemo had been successful but then learned it worked too well. The dead cancer cells had flooded into Mother's system and her kidneys couldn't keep up. They recommended dialysis, which seemed to destroy her body even more. My sisters, Daddy, and I prepared for the worst. We would gather around her bed talking and singing hymns and praying with her. Mother was a Christian, and we knew where she would spend eternity. However, she was far too young to be leaving us; the family needed her. But the disease was too strong and we lost my precious mother within a few more days.

I was shocked and wondered what God was thinking. How could He take my wonderful mother? People who worked with her said she was so kind and never talked about anyone. Everyone in our hometown of Haskell loved her. She was beautiful, inside and out, and had so much to give. Why did God let this happen? Bad things shouldn't happen to good people, right? Our family's world was forever changed. There is just something about losing one's mother. I don't think you ever get over it; you just have to live with it. And live with it we did, for a while.

As you might have guessed, we never rescheduled the counseling session and separated some months later. Again I was devastated. We were Christians, and divorce wasn't something you do. Besides, everyone had said we were the perfect couple. We had a great house, great jobs, and a great lifestyle traveling the world. We were active in the church and Bible Study. We just didn't have the 2.5 children the average family has—but no marriage is perfect.

Now I really did have sole responsibility for the home, so I hired a cleaning service from a coupon in the mail. I'd always been careful to obtain references for outside services and was very selective in my vendors. But my friends didn't seem to think references were critical if you utilized a reputable cleaning service. Well, this one wasn't; after one visit they came back when I was out of town and cleaned out my jewelry. My grandmother worked in a jewelry store and I had received a lot of jewelry throughout my life, some with incredible sentimental value—a watch when I graduated from high school, a ring when I graduated from college, earrings my mother splurged on one Christmas. Because of my travels, I also had unique pieces of jewelry from around the world—a cartouche from Cairo, sapphire earrings from Bangkok, a hand-hammered gold necklace from Indonesia. Plus, some beautiful items I'd inherited after my mother's passing. These were not just pieces of gold; they represented my life! How could someone do this to me?

I had great hopes for recovering the jewelry the first week or so after the theft. The police dusted for fingerprints, and I gave them the cleaning service's number and address. But the Houston police don't work the way the investigators do on CSI; they came up with nothing—or so they said. We later learned that the lab had mishandled evidence; I chose to believe mine was included. The police informed me they had bigger fish to fry. They said, "Too bad this didn't happen in a smaller town." I said, "In a smaller town I wouldn't have been robbed." I also wanted to say, "If my husband had been at home, this wouldn't have happened." At least that's the way I felt.

He was not too sympathetic when I called crying after the robbery. He reminded me that we aren't to "store up treasures on earth where moth and rust destroy, and where thieves break in and steal." I was pleased that he was quoting the Bible (Matthew 6:19) but it didn't make me feel any better. These were pieces of my life. The verse continues, "Store for yourself treasures in heaven…for where your treasure is, there your heart will be also." So where was my heart? I felt guilty bemoaning the loss of "things." After all, my mother had just passed away, and my husband and I were separated. Where was my heart? …It was broken.

The police were unable to find my treasures. I even searched pawn shops in hopes of identifying the pieces. I was told that the items were probably melted down the night of the robbery. What! My precious memories melted and sold. I had to remind myself they were only "things." But those things represented my mother and my family and my life. Still, I would have traded all the jewelry in the world for my mother to have lived—or for my husband and I to be together.

In the meantime, my firm was starting to become embroiled in some nasty publicity over the Enron scandal. The SEC was interrogating some of our partners and looking for a scapegoat on whom to blame the financial failure. Arthur Andersen had been the most prestigious of the big accounting firms and now was being accused of unethical behavior. It was unthinkable. We followed our lawyers' advice and provided everything the SEC asked for, but at the end of the day it was obvious they were out to make someone pay. We finally took our plight to the press and tried to rally public support. We were making progress, but it was too late. The SEC indicted the entire firm instead of the handful of people supposedly involved in the shredding of documents. Once our clients heard about the indictment, they felt they had an obligation to their shareholders to use someone more "ethical," regardless of what services we were providing or how much they valued us.

Again, the unimaginable was happening to me. My firm was going down and I would be left without a job, without the career at which I had worked hard to be a success. Talk about storing your treasures on earth! Well, at least now I had time to focus on the marriage. No more travel or long hours. But, again, it was too late. My marriage imploded along with my firm. It was like I had been run over by a truck and left on the street to bleed out.

I felt like Job when he lost everything—his family, his fortune, and his health. Friends told him to repent of his sins and ask for forgiveness, but Job said he was innocent. I knew I wasn't innocent, but I also wasn't totally to blame. Regardless, it was another loss, and I was wondering what was next. I didn't have to wait too long.

My grandmother passed away. Granted, she was 94 and, unlike my mother, had lived a full life. But the loss was still impactful. Grandmother had been a role model for me, strong and courageous, supporting herself my entire life. She had lots of hobbies, was active in the church and community, and devoted to us. When we were growing up, Grandmother would stop by to see us at least twice a day. When I worked at my uncle's Baptist encampment during my high-school summers, Grandmother wrote me a letter every day. I was the envy of the other workers. She continued to write me almost a letter a week for the rest of my life until she was unable to write. She was an amazing woman.

So I buried my beloved grandmother. A week later the divorce papers were signed. I had lost three of the most important people in my life. My family was shrinking before my eyes.

What was left? My house and my car? Again, possessions. Is that really what defines our lives? Had I fallen into that trap? Had my life been defined by my successes and my possessions? And now that I didn't have them I had no value?

I had definitely let my work define me. I had been a partner at Arthur Andersen, the elite of accounting firms, and now I was an unemployed accountess (female accountant). It didn't sound quite as impressive. I had lots of initials (CPA, CIA, CFE) to go with my name, but I'd lost the one that mattered most—MRS. It was embarrassing. How could you ruin a marriage with someone who loves you? I hear it happens all the time, but that doesn't give much comfort when it happens to you. And I had gone from two good incomes to no income. I felt I was giving Job a good run for his title.

I made the best use of my newfound time by working out and attending Bible studies almost every day—both relieved my stress and sadness. I still felt a combination of shame and anger and disbelief. Why did all these terrible things happen to me? I was a Christian and a great person. I had to keep reminding myself that my losses don't define me. God created me for a purpose, and my life still had value. I trusted in Jeremiah 29:11, "'For I know the plans I have for you,' declares the Lord, 'plans to prosper you and not to harm you, plans to give you hope and a future.'"

Have you ever suffered a loss and thought you couldn't go on or that you would never be the same again? You suffered a setback so financially or personally devastating that you wanted to give up. You wanted to raise your fist and cry out, "Why me, Lord?" We always want to know why. I eventually learned that the question I should have been asking is, "What can I take forward from this?" Not why, but what?

The Rolling Stones sang, "You can't always get what you want. You can't always get what you want. But if you try sometimes you just might find, you get what you need." I did have what I wanted, and it had been taken away from me. Now what I needed was to realize I was not the failure; that my losses were merely events I could overcome. God blessed me with time to heal, support from friends and my church, and comfort through His word. And I survived. It wasn't easy, but I survived, and eventually prospered just as Job did. I learned to cherish the memories instead of rue the losses. You can too.

What are you letting define you? Is it your career? Your spouse? Your house? Your car? Is it your assets or your accomplishments? If those things are defining you, like they did me, then their loss can make you feel a failure. However, as Zig Ziglar said, "It's not what happens to you that matters, it's how you respond to what happens to you that makes a difference." We have the opportunity to learn from our losses instead of letting them devastate us. That could mean spending more time with your loved ones or focusing on your relationships and not your possessions, or any number of lessons. What can we learn from the loss versus asking "Why me?"

Zig Ziglar also said, "Other things and other people can stop you temporarily. You're the only one who can do it permanently." Don't be the one to keep yourself from moving forward and growing. Observe and acknowledge what happened, allow your feelings to surface, get support from others, take responsibility for any role you had in the situation, forgive yourself and others, then let go and move on. These are the critical steps I took to move forward.

But the advice which helped me most was to have faith in God, regardless of the circumstances. Hebrews 13:5 states: "Never will I leave you; never will I forsake you." We can take comfort in knowing we are not alone, despite our losses. ▪

DEANNA SULLIVAN *An internationally recognized speaker, trainer and author, Deanna Sullivan has made it her mission to ensure that education is effective as well as fun. Her most popular topics are leadership, communication, ethics, and fraud. Her goal for every session is to educate, entertain, and motivate the participants to achieve their personal and professional goals. Deanna has a diverse background that ranges from auditing and accounting to consulting and training. She serves as chairman of the Houston Chapter of the Institute of Internal Auditors (IIA) annual conference, which attracts 1,200 participants, and was chairman of the IIA's highly rated 2006 International Conference, which attracted 2,500 people from around the globe. Deanna is certified to teach ethics for Texas CPAs and regularly receives comments such as, "The best ethics course I've ever attended!" Deanna recently was certified as a Ziglar Legacy Certified Trainer. Zig Ziglar was her hero, so she is delighted to be able to help carry his message around the world. Speaking is a passion of Deanna's, so when not traveling she teaches a Bible study class at Second Baptist Church in Houston, reads a weekly program, "Traveling Around," for Taping for the Blind, and is on the speakers committee for the Houston Livestock Show and Rodeo.*

Deanna Sullivan
5511 Beverlyhill Street
Houston TX 77056
deannasullivan@sbcglobal.net
Deannasullivan.com
713-780-8308

18

Don't Stop Yourself
Christa Trantham

Blue 42…Blue 42…Hut! Hut! It's the last 10 seconds of the game, no more time-outs, and it's fourth down. The Dallas Cowboys are down by three points. The offensive line sets up on the two-yard line to make the final, and hopefully game-winning, play. As the excitement builds… time almost stands still…the strong smell of hot dogs and beer permeate my nostrils…the hard plastic of the seat seems acutely harder than just a second ago…and all the sounds just fall away as the last play begins… Blue 42…Blue 42…Hut! Hut!

You can see every movement in slow motion as the play begins. First, the fake handoff to the running back, then the quarterback takes his almost patented "two-step drop-back"…scans the field…picks his target …and throws the ball. As the ball is moving through the air…the whole audience waits with baited breath…until it's suddenly obvious: There's no way the wide receiver—or anyone for that matter—is going to catch that ball. The game is lost.

What happened that day at Cowboy Stadium happens all the time in everyday life. Of course, hopefully, there aren't 80,000 people watching each time. In the final moments, when it really counts, the human machine—mental, physical, emotional—fails to succeed. The question on most people's minds in the aftermath following those moments is

"Why?" And while "Why?" may be the initial gut response, and at least a step in the right direction, the overriding question in my mind is "HOW DO WE STOP THAT?!"

It's amazing how much we relearn about life from our children. I have two young children who frequently afford me opportunities to learn and grow, especially when I'm paying attention. At age three, my youngest son, Aidan, gave me the gift of such an opportunity. My husband and I are big on teaching our children to be independent and how to politely speak their minds. So as I'm putting Aidan into his car seat, he spots a blue blanket in the other side of the car. He reaches out for the blanket and makes a small "umph" sound as his chest reaches the safety belt that I am busy fastening. He looks up at me and with his best effort says, "Mommy, will you please may you get the blanket for me?" Now that's not exactly proper English, but mommies understand these things. So I smiled and said, "I'd be happy to." THEN IT HAPPENED—my life lesson for the day! Aidan looks right in my eyes and says, "Please, don't stop yourself."

"Please, don't stop yourself." Those words reverberated in my head as I walked to the other side of the car to retrieve the blanket. How many times have we been happy to do something, or even excited to do something, and then let something internal stop us? How many times have we fully intended to follow through and then stopped ourselves along the way? How many times have we let something else divert and deter our best efforts in completing something good and meaningful? I was well on my way to contemplating this very thought as I handed the blanket to Aidan, and an excited voice came from inside the car, "Woo Hoo!"

My three-year-old had just reminded me of not only the importance of follow-through, but also the thrill of victory. Times like that make me glad to be a mommy. After all…

Each of us has the tendency to file away our successes into the deep recesses of our minds and just look at what else still needs to get done. Sometimes it's even worse; not only do we not look at the success, we look back and regret all the failures. Focusing on the unlimited "to do" list and/or looking backward with guilt over the unaccomplished does not create the fervent ground needed for success.

With greater and greater frequency, we need to allow ourselves to fully feel and appreciate the thrill of victory. Bask in the glory and happiness of the accomplishment! As you're reading this, take a second, pause, and think: When is the last time you really took time to look around at what you have accomplished in your business and appreciate yourself for those successes? Don't worry; it doesn't have to be an all-day affair. Just keep it in the top of your mind. Last year at TexInspec, the local home inspection company I help lead, we made tremendous progress. We hired and trained two new office people; we hired and trained a new inspector; we developed and set up two fully functional marketing programs; we systematized the process for bringing more customized materials to every presentation; we set up a better system for tracking marketing routes; and we grew almost 30 percent in revenue. Those are big accomplishments! But if we never look at them, I and my team might get lost in all the "to do" items we're currently working on. We might get discouraged by the size and audacity of the mission at hand.

It may seem obvious, but I want to make sure it's clear that we also need to ensure that we are following through to completion on the most important tasks—keeping ourselves focused on what is important and making sure that we are not stopping ourselves. My favorite way to do this is with a "Positive Focus" sheet, coupled with a short list I carry in my purse or pocket. Just keeping the most important tasks listed in front of you will redirect you to important tasks whenever distraction sets in. You can find the "Positive Focus" sheet and instructions at www.CoachBlue-print.com/IDareYou

Especially when starting a new project, the feeling of being overwhelmed tends to creep in as the "to do" list grows and the "done" list just gets passed over. I love the way Diane Lampe talks about her nightly routine of writing down what went right that day—so she can do more of it—and what could have gone better that day—so she can improve herself.

Make sure you're following through on the most important items on your list, the items that are building your future and helping you fulfill your life purpose. AND, just as importantly, make sure you're celebrating—at least in your own mind—the victories you accomplish each day.

I'm sure that…you, like me, have had inspirational moments that created a clear picture or action plan—something that seemed so obvious and so important that you knew it was right. What did you do the minute after that moment? Did the busy whirlwind of life, business, and "to do" items whoosh in and push the picture into oblivion? Or did it at least get you to agree to delay action? And did it in fact turn out to be delayed indefinitely?

Well, that's what's been happening to me. Over the past four months I have had one of those moments of clarity no less than six times, and on a singularly important topic: the mission, vision, values, and goals for our businesses. The first time the thought appeared, I quickly checked it off as already done. After all, we have a written vision; it's even framed and hanging on the wall in the office. We have a mission; we have values; and we have goals. So, initially, I made a mental note that, while it was a great idea, I had already done it.

The next time the message came through, it was a brief mention by a friend, just an everyday chat. So I reassured myself that we had already conquered outlining our mission, vision, values, and goals, and let the whirlwind of marketing, coaching, writing, and guiding others sweep away the idea entirely. The third time, I was actually starting to get annoyed. Why was my brain continually insisting on the importance of this already completed task? I am so grateful that God is willing to repeat Himself because by the fourth time, I was finally catching on. There was something unfinished or unrefined about how we had completed this task up to this point, and I needed to personally revisit and review these incredibly important guiding forces for our businesses.

Finally, I committed myself to dedicating the time and energy necessary to seriously revise and review our written mission, vision, values and goals. To me, this meant that each statement had to be clear and understood by every team member. So I've been doing strategic work on solidifying, clarifying, and quantifying our mission, vision, values, and goals for each of our companies. And one of the next great challenges in this step is communicating that to our amazing team—but that is a story for another time.

Focusing on this important and foundational yet transforming task has brought me closer to my "future me." "Future me" is the me that will be living my life in the future. You too have a "current you" and a "future you." No, I'm not suggesting that we're all schizophrenic—although some days I wonder (*grin*). I just have a really good grasp of how I perceive me. Allow me to explain: Every time you think of a task or an outcome, you picture it with either "current you" eyes or "future you" eyes. Current you is frequently subject to everything that's going on right now in your life. Current you is acutely aware of how little sleep you got last night. Current you is painfully aware of the last promise to yourself that you didn't keep. Current you is hungry, agitated, desirous of that new toy you want, and so on.

"Future you" is entirely different. Future you is how you view yourself in the future. Research shows that most people view their future self much differently than their current self. They imagine their future self to have less stress and fewer "to do" items. This is one of the main reasons they choose to put off starting or finishing projects until later. It is the "future self" disconnect that triggers buying that expensive TV instead of investing in their education, deciding to start losing weight next Monday, for example. In other words, they have an idealized picture of their future self and are not in tune with the needs and desires of their future self.

The harsh reality is that "future you" needs you to act right—and right now. Future you needs current you to get your tookis in gear. Make sure your business is supporting your family now and will continue to support your family in the future. Future you needs current you to realize that you will also have sleepless nights, stressful situations, and life in general to deal with. You need to make sure you're taking care of business today—and smartly so—to help protect and provide for future you.

Being in tune with your future you and feeling a closeness and co-maradery with future you significantly increases the value of your daily decisions. It makes you more willing to act despite a less-than-perfect day—or even a significantly less-than-perfect day. It makes you more likely to invest in yourself both in saving and education, providing future you with the tools and knowledge to fulfill your passion and your life's ambition.

One great way to get closer to future you is "future pacing." This is a neat activity that really helps you focus on what you want in life. "Future pacing" involves creating an extremely detailed plan and vision for your future life. This plan can be and really is best served by being a little rosy and exciting; this plan and vision needs to take into account the things you'll need in order to create that rosy picture. Create vivid closeness with the future you using all five of your senses. As you draw your future in your mind's eye, make sure to fully communicate with all of your body and mind. Take the time to really feel what that future life will feel like both in the physical world and also in the emotional world. Take the time to identify and become desirous of the smells, sounds, sights, and even the tastes of the future life. Now, further enhance and activate your future vision by clearly involving the analytical part of your brain as well by envisioning numbers and percentages and how a plan might actually come together to make this future vision a reality. Make sure your vision is a crisp and clear picture of events and items in your life. Every day, take a few minutes and bring up that future you picture. As you age, the future you envision will change—and that's good.

One great way to become more in tune with your future self is to better define your mission, vision, values, and goals. AND—and this is a HUGE AND!—tell at least one other person what your mission, vision, values, and goals are. By telling even one other person about your mission, you receive the gift of hearing yourself voice your mission to someone else. Not only does it provide you with additional clarity, just hearing it out loud helps reinforce your commitment; and when you tell someone else, you're also blessed with additional encouragement to succeed.

I look forward to hearing many "Future You" stories from the "Current You" soon! ▪

CHRISTA TRANTHAM. *Do you feel like you're doing what you were born to do? Christa Trantham's personal purpose is to "Help People Help Themselves and Others"—and she does just that every day of the week. Christa began working in her father's small business every summer at the young and impressionable age of 12 years old. She quickly found out how exhilarating it felt to be part of a small business and to help it grow—well, let's just say she never looked back. She dedicated herself to small-business success, and yes, for herself, but also for others!*

Between completing her degree in marketing at the University of Texas at Arlington and working full-time in a small business, she grew in the experience and wisdom needed to succeed and to help others succeed. Today, as co founder of Coach Blueprint and business manager for Millionaire Inspector Community and TexInspec, Christa leads both small and large groups to personal and professional significance.

We all need a great person in our life who is…Efficient, Strategic, Down to Earth, Highly Practical, and occasionally—BLUNT! Christa Trantham is that person.

Christa Trantham
CoachBlueprint@MikeCrow.com
888-566-5993

CPSIA information can be obtained at www.ICGtesting.com
Printed in the USA
LVOW13s0116050814

397423LV00003BA/4/P